JUST LIKE MUM USED TO MAKE

SOUPS

JUST LIKE MUM USED TO MAKE

SOUPS

National Trust

First published in the United Kingdom in 2009 by
Collins & Brown
An imprint of Anova Books Company Ltd
10 Southcombe Street
London W14 0RA

This edition published for W H Smith in 2014

ISBN 9781907892899

A catalogue record for this book is available from the British Library.

20 19 18 17 16 15 14
7 6 5 4 3 2 1

Printed by CT Printing, China

NOTES
• Both metric and imperial measures are given for the recipes. Follow either set of measures, not
a mixture of both, as they are not interchangeable.
• All spoon measures are level.
1 tsp = 5ml spoon; 1 tbsp = 15ml spoon.
• Ovens and grills must be preheated to the specified temperature.
• Use sea salt and freshly ground black pepper unless otherwise suggested.
• Fresh herbs should be used unless dried herbs are specified in a recipe.
• Medium eggs should be used except where otherwise specified. Free-range eggs are
recommended.
• Note that certain recipes, including mayonnaise, lemon curd and some cold desserts, contain
raw or lightly cooked eggs. The young, elderly, pregnant women and anyone with an immune-
deficiency disease should avoid these, because of the slight risk
of salmonella.
• Calorie, fat and carbohydrate counts per serving are provided for the recipes.
• If you are following a gluten- or dairy-free diet, check the labels on all pre-packaged food
goods.
• Nutritional information for serving suggestions do not take gluten- or dairy-free diets into
account.

Picture credits
Photographers: Neil Barclay (page 103); Nicki Dowey (47, 55, 57, 59, 61, 65, 67, 68, 71, 73, 75,
77, 79, 89, 91, 93, 95, 99, 101, 105, 107, 109, 113, 115, 117, 119, 121, 123, 125, 127, 129, 131,
133, 137, 139, 143, 145, 147, 151, 153, 155, 157, 159, 161, 163, 169, 173, 175, 179, 181, 185,
189); Craig Robertson (Basics photography plus pages 49, 51, 53, 63, 83, 85, 87, 97, 115, 119,
167, 177, 187); Lucinda Symons (pages, 5 41, 149, 183).

Contents

The Basics

Making soups

Soups are nutritious, full of flavour and easy to make. Incredibly versatile, they can be smooth or chunky, light for a first course or substantial for a main course, made with vegetables, pulses, meat, chicken or fish.

Puréeing soups

1. Using a jug blender: Allow the soup to cool slightly, then fill the jug about half-full, making sure that there is more liquid than solids. Cover the lid with a teatowel and hold it on tightly. Blend until smooth, then add more solids and blend again until all the soup is smooth. (If you have a lot of soup, transfer each batch to a clean pan.)

2. Using a stick blender: Allow the soup to cool slightly. Stick the blender deep into the soup, switch it on and then move it about so that all the soup is puréed.
   Note: Don't do this in a non-stick pan.

3. Using a mouli: A mouli-légumes makes a fine purée, although it takes a little longer than using a blender. Fit the fine plate to the mouli-légumes and set it over a bowl – put a teatowel underneath to keep it from moving on the table. Fill the bowl of the mouli about halfway up the sides, putting in more solids than liquid. Work in batches if you have a large quantity of soup.

4. Using a sieve: If you don't have a blender or mouli-légumes, you can purée soup by just pushing it through a sieve, although this will take a much longer time.

Partially puréed soups

1. To give a soup a more interesting texture, you can purée just one-third to half of the ingredients, and then stir the purée back into the soup before reheating at the end.

2. Alternatively, prepare the vegetables or the other ingredients, but set aside a few choice pieces. While the soup is cooking, steam or boil these pieces until they are just tender; refresh green vegetables in cold water. Just before serving, cut into smaller pieces and add to the soup.

1 2
3 4

Simple Vegetable Soup

You can use almost any mixture of vegetables in this soup. To serve 4 people, you will need:

1 or 2 finely chopped onions, 2 tbsp oil or 1 tbsp oil and 25g (1oz) butter, 1 or 2 crushed garlic cloves (optional), 450g (1lb) chopped mixed vegetables, such as leeks, potatoes, celery, fennel, canned tomatoes and parsnips (chopped finely or cut into larger dice for a chunky soup), 1.1 litres (2 pints) stock.

1. Fry the onions in the oil or oil and butter until soft and add the garlic if you like.

2. Add the chopped mixed vegetables and stock. Bring to the boil. Simmer for 20–30 minutes until the vegetables are tender.

3. Leave the soup chunky, partially purée or blend until smooth.

Chunky soups

1. Cut the ingredients into bite-size pieces. Heat oil or butter in the soup pan and cook the onions – and garlic if you like – until soft and lightly coloured.

2. Add the remaining ingredients, putting in those that need the longest cooking first. Pour in some stock and bring to the boil.

3. Simmer gently until all the ingredients are tender. If too much liquid boils away, you can just add a little more.

Making stock

Good stock can make the difference between a good soup and a great one. It also gives depth of flavour to many dishes. There are four main types of stock: vegetable, meat, chicken and fish.

Vegetable Stock

For 1.2 litres (2 pints), you will need:

225g (8oz) each onions, celery, leeks and carrots, chopped, 1 bouquet garni (2 bay leaves, a few thyme sprigs, 1 small bunch of parsley), 10 black peppercorns, ½ tsp salt.

1 Put all the ingredients into a large pan and add 1.7 litres (3 pints) cold water. Bring slowly to the boil and skim the surface.

2 Partially cover the pan and simmer for 30 minutes. Adjust the seasoning if necessary. Strain the stock through a fine sieve into a bowl and leave to cool.

Meat Stock

For 900ml (1½ pints), you will need:

450g (1lb) each meat bones and stewing meat, 1 onion, 2 celery sticks and 1 large carrot, sliced, 1 bouquet garni (2 bay leaves, a few thyme sprigs, 1 small bunch of parsley), 1 tsp black peppercorns, ½ tsp salt.

1 Preheat the oven to 220°C (200°C fan oven) mark 7. Put the meat and bones into a roasting tin and roast in the oven for about 30–40 minutes, turning now and again, until they are well browned.

2 Put the bones into a large saucepan with the remaining ingredients and then add 2 litres (3½ pints) cold water. Bring slowly to the boil and skim the surface.

3 Partially cover the pan and simmer gently for 4–5 hours. Adjust the seasoning if necessary. Strain through a muslin-lined sieve into a bowl and cool quickly. Degrease (see page 15) before using the stock.

Cook's Tips

- To get a clearer liquid when you are making fish, meat or poultry stock, all you need do is strain the cooked stock through four layers of muslin in a sieve.

- Stock will keep for three days in the refrigerator. If you want to keep it for a further three days, transfer it to a pan and reboil gently for five minutes. Cool, put in a clean bowl and chill for a further three days.

- When you are making meat or chicken stock, make sure there is a good ratio of meat to bones. The more meat you use, the more flavour the stock will have.

Chicken Stock

For 1.2 litres (2 pints), you will need:

1.6kg (3½lb) chicken bones, 225g (8oz) each onions and celery, sliced, 150g (5oz) chopped leeks, 1 bouquet garni (2 bay leaves, a few thyme sprigs, 1 small bunch of parsley), 1 tsp black peppercorns, ½ tsp salt.

1. Put all the ingredients into a large pan and add 3 litres (5¼ pints) cold water. Bring slowly to the boil and skim the surface.

2. Partially cover the pan and simmer gently for 2 hours. Adjust the seasoning if necessary.

3. Strain the stock through a muslin-lined sieve into a bowl and cool quickly. Degrease (see opposite) before using the stock.

Fish Stock

For 900ml (1½ pints), you will need:

900g (2lb) fish bones and trimmings, washed, 2 carrots, 1 onion and 2 celery sticks, sliced, 1 bouquet garni (2 bay leaves, a few thyme sprigs, 1 small bunch of parsley), 6 white peppercorns, ½ tsp salt.

1. Put all the ingredients into a large saucepan and add 900ml (1½ pints) cold water. Bring slowly to the boil and skim the surface.

2. Partially cover the pan and simmer gently for 30 minutes. Adjust the seasoning if necessary.

3. Strain through a muslin-lined sieve into a bowl and cool quickly. Fish stock tends not to have much fat in it and so does not usually need to be degreased. However, if it does seem to be fatty, you will need to remove this by degreasing it (see opposite).

Degreasing stock

Meat and poultry stock needs to be degreased. (Vegetable stock does not.) You can mop the fat from the surface using some absorbent kitchen paper, but the following methods are easier and more effective. There are three main methods that you can use: ladling, pouring and chilling.

1 Ladling: While the stock is warm, place a ladle on the surface. Press down and allow the fat floating on the surface to trickle over the edge until the ladle is full. Discard the fat, then repeat until all the fat has been removed.

2 Pouring: For this you need a degreasing jug or a double-pouring gravy boat, which has the spout at the base of the vessel. When you fill the jug or gravy boat with a fatty liquid, the fat rises. When you pour, the stock comes out while the fat stays behind in the jug.

3 Chilling: This technique works best with stock that is made from meat, as the fat solidifies when the stock is cold. Put the stock in the refrigerator until the fat becomes solid, then remove the pieces of fat using a slotted spoon.

Preparing vegetables

Vegetables form the basis of most soups – whether smooth or chunky – adding flavour and bulk. Here are some of the most popular vegetables and how to prepare them.

Onions

1 Cut off the tip and base of the onion, then peel away all the layers of papery skin and any discoloured layers underneath.

2 Put the onion, root end down, on a chopping board, then, using a sharp knife, cut the onion in half from tip to base.

3 Slicing: Put one half of the onion on the board with the cut surface facing down and then slice across the onion.

4 Chopping: Slice the halved onions from the root end to the top at regular intervals. Next, make 2–3 horizontal slices through the onion, then slice vertically across the width.

Shallots

1 Cut off the tip and trim off the ends of the root. Peel off the skin and any discoloured layers underneath.

2 Holding the shallot with the root end down, use a small, sharp knife to make deep parallel slices almost down to the base while keeping the slices attached to it.

3 Slicing: Turn the shallot on its side and cut off slices from the base.

4 Dicing: Make some deep parallel slices at right angles to the first slices. Turn the shallot on its side and cut off the slices from the base. You should now have fine dice, but chop any larger pieces individually.

Peeling tomatoes

1. Fill a bowl or saucepan with boiling water. Using a slotted spoon, carefully add the tomato and leave for 15–30 seconds, then remove to a chopping board.

2. Use a small sharp knife to cut out the core in a single cone-shaped piece. Discard the core.

3. Peel off the skin; it should come away easily, depending on ripeness.

Seeding tomatoes

1. Halve the tomato through the core. Use a spoon or a small sharp knife to remove the seeds and juice. Shake off the excess liquid.

2. Chop the tomato as required for your recipe and place in a colander for a minute or two, to drain off any excess liquid.

Cutting tomatoes

1. Use a small sharp knife to cut out the core in a single cone-shaped piece. Discard the core.

2. Wedges: Halve the tomato and then cut into quarters or into three.

3. Slices: Hold the tomato with the cored side on the chopping board for greater stability and use a serrated knife to cut into slices.

Seeding peppers

The seeds and white pith of peppers taste bitter, so they should be removed.

1. Cut off the top of the pepper, and then cut away and discard the seeds and white pith.

2. Alternatively, cut the pepper in half vertically and snap out the white pithy core and seeds. Trim away the rest of the white membrane with a knife.

Chargrilling peppers

Charring imparts a wonderful smoky flavour and makes peppers much easier to peel.

1. Hold the pepper, using tongs, over the gas flame on your hob (or under a preheated grill) until the skin blackens, turning until black all over.

2. Put into a bowl, cover and leave to cool (the steam will help to loosen the skin). Peel.

Carrots

1. First, peel and cut off the ends of the carrot. Cut slices off each of the rounded sides to make four flat surfaces that are stable on the chopping board.

2. Hold the carrot pieces steady with one hand and cut lengthways into even slices so they are lying in a flat stack.

3. To dice the shreds, turn the stack at right angles and then carrefully cut through in the opposite direction.

Mushrooms

Whether they are button, white, chestnut or flat mushrooms, they are all prepared in a similar way.

1   Wipe with a damp cloth or pastry brush to remove any dirt.

2   With button mushrooms, cut off the stalk flush with the base of the cap. For other mushrooms, cut a thin disc off the end of the stalk and discard. Chop or slice the mushrooms.

Squash

1 For steaming, baking or roasting, keep the chunks fairly large – at least 2.5cm (1in) thick. Peel the squash with a swivel-handled peeler or a chef's knife.

2 Halve the squash, then use a knife to cut through some of the fibrous mass connecting the seeds with the wall of the central cavity. Scoop out the seeds and fibres with a spoon, then cut the flesh into pieces.

Leeks

As some leeks harbour a lot of grit and earth between their leaves, they need careful cleaning.

1 Cut off the root and any tough parts of the leek. Make a cut into the leaf end of the leek, about 7.5cm (3in) deep.

2 Hold the leek under the cold tap while separating the cut halves to expose any grit. Wash well, then shake dry. Use the green tops for stock.

Cabbage

The crinkly leaved Savoy cabbage may need more washing than other varieties, because its open leaves catch dirt more easily than the tightly packed white and red cabbage. The following method is suitable for all cabbages.

1. Pick off any of the outer leaves that are dry, tough or discoloured. Cut off the base and, using a small sharp knife, cut out as much as possible of the tough inner core in a single cone-shaped piece.

2. If you need whole cabbage leaves, peel them off one by one. As you work your way down, you will need to cut out more of the core.

3. If you are cooking the cabbage in wedges, cut it in half lengthways then cut the pieces into wedges of the required size.

Asparagus

Cut or snap off the woody stem of each asparagus spear about 5cm (2in) from the stalk end, or where the white and green sections meet. Or cut off the stalk end and then peel with a vegetable peeler or small sharp knife.

Courgettes

Cutting diagonally is an ideal, all-purpose shape if you are using courgettes as a garnish for soup.

1. After washing under the cold tap, dry the courgette well and trim the base and the stem.

2. Trim off a piece at the base at a 45 degree angle, then repeat with the remaining courgette.

Avocados

Prepare avocados just before using in a soup because their flesh discolours quickly once it is exposed to the air.

1. Halve the avocado lengthways and twist the two halves apart. Tap the stone with a sharp knife, then twist to remove the stone.

2. Run a knife between the flesh and skin and pull away. Slice or chop the flesh as required.

Spring onions

Cut off the roots and trim any coarse or withered green parts. Slice diagonally, or shred by cutting into 5cm (2in) lengths and then slicing down the lengths, or chop finely, according to the recipe.

Fennel

■ Trim off the top stems and the base of the fennel bulbs. Remove the core with a small sharp knife if it seems tough.

② The outer leaves may be discoloured and can be scrubbed gently in cold water, or you can peel away the discoloured parts with a knife or a vegetable peeler. Slice the fennel or cut it into quarters, according to your recipe.

Broccoli

■ Slice off the end of the stalk and cut 1cm (½in) below the florets.

② Peel the thick, woody skin from the stalks and slice in half or quarters lengthways. Cut off equal-sized florets with a small knife. If the florets are very large you can halve them by cutting lengthways through the stalk and pulling the two halves apart.

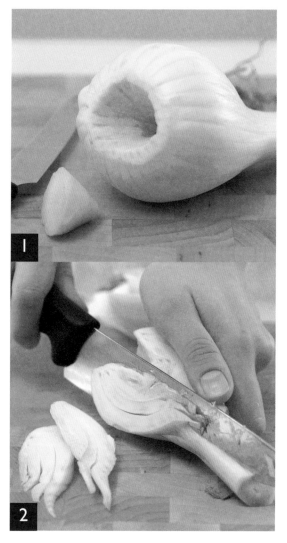

Using herbs

Most herbs are the leaf of a flowering plant, and are usually sold with much of the stalk intact. They have to be washed, trimmed and then chopped or torn into pieces that are suitable for your recipe.

Washing

1. Trim the roots and part of the stalks from the herbs. Immerse in cold water and shake briskly. Leave in the water for a few minutes.

2. Lift out of the water and place in a colander or sieve, then rinse again under the cold tap. Leave to drain for a few minutes and then dry thoroughly on kitchen paper or teatowels, or use a salad spinner.

Chopping

1. Trim the herbs by pinching off all but the smallest, most tender stalks. If the herb is one with a woody stalk, such as rosemary or thyme, it may be easier to remove the leaves by rubbing the whole bunch between your hands; the leaves should simply pull off the stems.

2. If you are chopping the leaves, gather them into a compact ball in one hand, keeping your fist around the ball (but being careful not to crush them).

3. Chop with a large knife, using a rocking motion and letting just a little of the ball out of your fingers at a time.

4. When the herbs are roughly chopped, continue chopping until the pieces are in small shreds or flakes.

Flavourings

Garlic, ginger and spring onions are the basic flavourings in many soups, especially the spicier ones. Many of these soups also include chillies, lemongrass or a prepared spice paste such as Thai curry paste.

Ginger

1 Grating: Cut off a piece of the root and peel with a vegetable peeler. Cut off any brown spots.

2 Rest the grater on a chopping board or small plate and grate the ginger. Discard any large fibres adhering to the pulp.

3 Slicing, shredding and chopping: Cut slices off the ginger and cut off the skin carefully. Cut off any brown spots. Stack the slices and then cut into shreds. To chop, stack the shreds and cut across into small pieces.

4 Pressing: If you just need the ginger juice, peel and cut off any brown spots, then cut into small chunks and use a garlic press held over a small bowl to extract the juice.

Lemongrass

Lemongrass is a popular South-east Asian ingredient, giving an aromatic lemony flavour. It looks rather like a long, slender spring onion, but is fibrous and woody and is usually removed before the dish is served.

Alternatively, the inner leaves may be very finely sliced, chopped or even pounded in a mortar and pestle and used in soups and spice pastes. Dried and powdered versions of lemongrass are also available.

Garlic

1 Put the clove on a chopping board and place the flat side of a large knife on top of it. Press down firmly on the flat of the blade to crush the clove and break the papery skin.

2 Cut off the base of the clove and then slip the garlic out of its skin – it should come away really easily.

3 Slicing: Using a rocking motion with the knife tip on the chopping board, slice the garlic as thinly as you need.

4 Shredding and chopping: Holding the slices together, shred them across the slices. Chop the shreds if you need chopped garlic.

5 Crushing: After step 2, the whole clove can be put into a garlic press. To crush with a knife: roughly chop the peeled cloves with a pinch of salt. Press down hard with the edge of a large knife tip (with the blade facing away from you), then drag the blade along the garlic while still pressing hard. Continue to do this, dragging the knife tip over the garlic.

Chillies

1 Cut off the cap and slit the chilli open lengthways. Using a spoon, scrape out the seeds and the pith.

2 For diced chilli, cut into thin shreds lengthways, then cut crossways.

Cook's Tip

Wash hands thoroughly after handling chillies – the volatile oils will sting if accidentally rubbed into your eyes.

Spices and sauces

Most aromatic spices are sold dried, either whole or ground. For optimum flavour, you should always buy whole spices and then grind them yourself.

Spices

Cayenne pepper is made from small, hot dried red chillies. It is always sold ground and is sweet, pungent and extremely hot. Use it very sparingly. Unlike paprika, cayenne pepper cannot be used for colouring as its flavour is too pronounced.

Chilli, available as powder or flakes as well as fresh, is a fiery hot spice and should be used cautiously. Some brands, often called mild chilli powder or chilli seasoning, are a mixture of chilli and other flavourings, such as cumin, oregano, salt and garlic; these are therefore considerably less fiery than hot chilli powder. Adjust the quantity you use accordingly.

Cinnamon is the dried, rolled bark of a tropical evergreen tree. Available as sticks as well as in powdered form, it has a sweet, pungent flavour. Cinnamon sticks have a more pronounced flavour than the powder, but they are quite difficult to grind at home, so always buy ready-ground cinnamon for use in sweet, spicy baking. Use cinnamon sticks to flavour meat casseroles, vegetable dishes, chutneys and pickles.

Coriander seeds have a mild, sweet, orangey flavour and they taste quite different from the fresh green leaves, which are used as a herb. Sold whole or ground, they are a common ingredient of most curry powders.

Cumin has a strong, slightly bitter taste, which is improved by toasting. Sold whole as seeds, or ground, it is an ingredient of curry powders and some chilli powder mixtures.

Curry leaves These shiny leaves have a fresh-tasting flavour akin to curry powder. They are used as a herb in cooking, most often added whole, but sometimes chopped first. The fresh or dried leaves

Which oil to use?

Groundnut (peanut) oil has a mild flavour and is well suited to stir-frying and deep-frying as it has a high smoke point and can therefore be used at high temperatures.

Sesame oil has a distinctive nutty flavour; it is best used in marinades or added as a seasoning to stir-fried dishes just before serving.

Vegetable oil may be pure cold-pressed rapeseed oil, sunflower oil, or a blend of corn, soya bean, rapeseed or other oils. It usually has a bland flavour and is suitable for stir-frying.

Coconut milk
Canned coconut milk is widely available, but if you can't find it, use blocks of creamed coconut or coconut powder, following the packet instructions to make the amount of liquid you need.

can be used sparingly to flavour soups and stews. Sold fresh in bunches in specialist Asian stores, curry leaves can be frozen in a plastic bag, kept in the freezer and added to dishes as required.

Fenugreek seeds are yellow-brown and very hard, with a distinctive aroma and slightly harsh, hot flavour. An ingredient of commercial curry powders, fenugreek is also used in chutneys, pickles and sauces.

Nutmeg, the seed of the nutmeg fruit, has a distinctive, nutty flavour. It is sold either whole or ground, but is best bought whole since the flavour of freshly grated nutmeg is far superior.

Paprika is a sweet mild spice made from certain varieties of red pepper; it is always sold ground to a red powder. It is good for adding colour to pale egg and cheese dishes. Some varieties, particularly Hungarian, are hotter than others. Paprika doesn't keep its flavour well, so buy this spice little and often. Produced from oak-smoked red peppers, smoked paprika has an intense flavour and a wonderful smoky aroma. Sweet, bittersweet and hot-smoked varieties are available.

Spice mixes
Curry powder: Bought curry powders are readily available, but for optimum flavour make your own. To make your own curry powder: jst put 1 tbsp each cumin and fenugreek seeds, ½ tsp mustard seeds, 1½ tsp each poppy seeds, black peppercorns and ground ginger, 4 tbsp coriander seeds, ½ tsp hot chilli powder and 2 tbsp ground turmeric into an electric blender or grinder. Grind to a fine powder. Store the curry powder in an airtight container and use within one month.

Garam masala: Sold ready-prepared, this Indian spice mix is aromatic rather than hot. To make your own garam masala at home: grind together 10 green cardamom pods, 1 tbsp black peppercorns and 2 tsp cumin seeds. Store in an airtight container and use within one month.

Saffron, the most expensive of all spices, is the dried stigma of the saffron crocus flower. It has a wonderful subtle flavour and aroma and imparts a hint of yellow to the foods it is cooked with. Powdered saffron is available, but it is the whole stigmas, called saffron strands or threads, that give the best results. A generous pinch is all that is needed to flavour and colour dishes.

Turmeric is a member of the ginger family though it is rarely available fresh. The bright orange root is commonly dried, then ground and sold as powder. Turmeric powder has an aromatic, slightly bitter flavour and should be used sparingly in curry powder, pickles and rice dishes. Like saffron, turmeric colours the foods it is cooked with, but it has a much harsher flavour than saffron.

Thai green curry paste is a blend of spices, such as green chillies, coriander and lemongrass. Thai red curry paste contains fresh and dried red chillies and ginger. Once opened, store in a sealed container in the refrigerator.

Sauces

Soy sauce – made from fermented soya beans and, usually, wheat, this is the most common flavouring in Chinese and South-east Asian cooking. There are light and dark versions of soy sauce; the dark kind is slightly sweeter and tends to darken the food. It will keep indefinitely.

Tabasco – a fiery hot sauce based on red chillies, spirit vinegar and salt, and prepared to a secret recipe. A dash of Tabasco may be used to add a kick to soups, casseroles, sauces, rice dishes and tomato-based drinks.

Thai fish sauce – a salty condiment with a distinctive, pungent aroma. It is used in many South-east Asian dishes. You can buy it in most large supermarkets and Asian food stores. It will keep indefinitely.

Using beans and lentils

Many dried beans and peas need to be soaked overnight before cooking. Lentils do not need soaking and are quicker to cook. Quicker still are canned beans: they are ready to use, but should be drained in a sieve and rinsed in cold water first.

Cooking beans

1 Pick through the beans to remove any grit or stones. Put the beans in a bowl or pan and pour over cold water to cover generously. Leave to soak for at least 8 hours, then drain. (Or pour boiling water over and leave the beans to cool in the water for 1–2 hours.)

2 Put the soaked beans into a large pan and add cold water to cover by at least 5cm (2in). Bring to the boil and boil rapidly for 10 minutes.

3 Skim off the scum that rises to the top, reduce the heat and leave to simmer until the beans are soft inside. They should be tender but not falling apart. Check periodically to make sure there's enough water to keep the beans well covered. Drain well. If using in a salad, allow to cool completely.

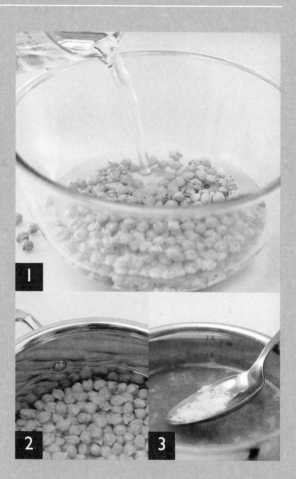

Cooking times

Older beans take longer to cook, so check their 'best before' date. For some pulses, such as red kidney beans, aduki beans, black-eyed beans, black beans and borlotti beans, it is essential to cover them with fresh cold water, bring to the boil and boil rapidly for 10 minutes to destroy any toxins. Then you can reduce the heat and and cook at a steady simmer for the following times:

Chickpeas	1–2 hours
Cannellini, borlotti, butter, flageolet, red kidney beans	1–3 hours
Red lentils	20 minutes
Green lentils	30–40 minutes

Simple Soup Garnishes

Toasted Croûtons

1. Cut the crusts off sliced white bread, then cut into dice 1–2cm (½ –¾in) square. Put the bread on a baking sheet and drizzle lightly with oil, then toss well with your hands.

2. Spread the bread dice out in a single layer and bake at 200°C (180°C fan oven) mark 6 for 8–10 minutes until lightly browned.

Fried Croûtons

Croûtons fried in a generous amount of oil will crispen all over and be appetisingly golden.

1. Cut the crusts off sliced white bread, then cut into dice 1–2cm (½ –¾in) square.

2. Heat the oil medium-hot in a frying pan. Fry in a single layer, stirring constantly, until brown all over. Drain on kitchen paper.

Fresh Herbs

A simple sprinkling of fresh snipped herbs makes a delicious garnish for soups. Fresh herb flowers can also make a pretty and unusual garnish.

Chop the herbs just before serving, and choose a herb that complements that flavour of soup – for example, basil with tomato, chives with creamy soups, or coriander with Asian-style soups.

Cream

Cream and other dairy products such as yogurt and crème fraîche can also make a simple garnish, drizzled or spooned on to soup just before serving. They also add body and texture, so use sparingly if the soup already includes cream.

Food storage and hygiene

Storing food properly and preparing it in a hygienic way is extremely important to ensure that food remains as nutritious and flavourful as possible, and to reduce the risk of food poisoning.

Hygiene

When you are preparing food, always follow these important guidelines:

Wash your hands thoroughly before handling food and again between handling different types of food, such as raw and cooked meat and poultry. If you have cuts or grazes on your hands, be sure to keep them covered with a waterproof plaster.

Wash down worksurfaces regularly with a mild detergent solution or multi-surface cleaner.

Use a dishwasher if available. Otherwise, wear rubber gloves for washing-up, so that the water temperature can be hotter than unprotected hands can bear. Change drying-up cloths and cleaning cloths regularly. Note that leaving dishes to drain is far more hygienic than drying them with a teatowel.

Keep raw and cooked foods separate, especially meat, fish and poultry. Wash kitchen utensils in between preparing raw and cooked foods. Never put cooked or ready-to-eat foods directly on to a surface that has just had raw fish, meat or poultry on it.

Keep pets out of the kitchen if possible; or make sure they stay away from worksurfaces. Never allow animals on to worksurfaces.

Shopping

Always choose fresh ingredients in prime condition from stores and markets that have a regular turnover of stock to ensure you buy the freshest produce possible.

Make sure items are within their 'best before' or 'use by' date. (Foods with a longer shelf life have a 'best before' date; more perishable items have a 'use by' date.)

Pack frozen and chilled items in an insulated cool bag at the check-out and then put them into the freezer or refrigerator as soon as you get home.

During warm weather in particular, always buy any perishable foods just before you return home. When packing items at the check-out, sort them according to where you will store them when you get home, such as the refrigerator, freezer, storecupboard, vegetable rack, fruit bowl, etc. This will make unpacking easier – and quicker.

The storecupboard

Although storecupboard ingredients will generally last a long time, correct storage is important:

- **Always check packaging** for storage advice – even with familiar foods, because storage requirements may change if additives, sugar or salt have been reduced.

- **Check storecupboard foods** for their 'best before' or 'use by' date and do not use them if the date has passed.

- **Keep all food cupboards scrupulously clean** and make sure food containers and packets are properly sealed.

■ **Once opened, treat canned foods as though fresh.** Transfer the contents to a clean container, cover and keep in the refrigerator. Similarly, jars, sauce bottles and cartons should be kept chilled after opening. (Check the label for safe storage times after opening.)

■ **Transfer dry goods** such as sugar, flour, rice and pasta to moisture-proof containers. When supplies are used up, wash the container well and thoroughly dry before refilling with new supplies.

■ **Store oils** in a dark cupboard away from any heat source as heat and light can make them turn rancid and affect their colour. For the same reason, buy olive oil in dark green bottles.

■ **Store vinegars** in a cool place; they can turn bad in a warm environment.

■ **Store dried herbs, spices and flavourings** in a cool, dark cupboard or in dark jars. Buy in small quantities as their flavour will not last indefinitely.

Refrigerator storage

Fresh food needs to be kept in the cool temperature of the refrigerator to keep it in good condition and discourage the growth of harmful bacteria. Store day-to-day perishable items, such as opened jams and jellies, mayonnaise and bottled sauces, in the refrigerator along with eggs and dairy products, fruit juices, bacon, fresh and cooked meat (on separate shelves), and salads and vegetables (except potatoes, which don't suit being stored in the cold). A refrigerator should be kept at an operating temperature of 4–5°C. It is worth investing in a refrigerator thermometer to ensure the correct temperature is maintained.

To ensure your refrigerator is functioning effectively for safe food storage, follow these guidelines:

- **To avoid bacterial cross-contamination**, store cooked and raw foods on separate shelves, putting cooked foods on the top shelf. Ensure that all items are well wrapped.

- **Never put hot food** into the refrigerator, as this will cause the internal temperature of the refrigerator to rise.

- **Avoid overfilling** the refrigerator, as this restricts the circulation of air and prevents the appliance from working properly.

- **It can take time** for the refrigerator to return to the correct operating temperature once the door has been opened, so don't leave it open any longer than is necessary.

- **Clean the refrigerator** regularly, using a specially formulated germicidal refrigerator cleaner. Or use a weak solution of bicarbonate of soda: 1 tbsp to 1 litre (1¾ pints) water.

- **If your refrigerator** doesn't have an automatic defrost facility, defrost regularly.

Maximum refrigerator storage times

For pre-packed foods, always adhere to the 'use by' date on the packet. For other foods the following storage times should apply, providing the food is in prime condition when it goes into the refrigerator and that your refrigerator is in good working order:

Vegetables and Fruit

Green vegetables	3–4 days
Salad leaves	2–3 days
Hard and stone fruit	3–7 days
Soft fruit	1–2 days

Dairy Food

Cheese, hard	1 week
Cheese, soft	2–3 days
Eggs	1 week
Milk	4–5 days

Raw Meat

Bacon	7 days
Game	2 days
Minced meat	1 day
Offal	1 day
Poultry	2 days
Raw sliced meat	2 days.

Cooked Meat

Sliced meat	2 days
Ham	2 days
Ham, vacuum-packed (or according to the instructions on the packet)	1–2 weeks

Smooth and creamy

Parsnip Soup with Chorizo

40g (1½oz) butter
1 onion, roughly chopped
225g (8oz) floury potatoes, such as
King Edward, peeled and chopped
400g (14oz) parsnips, peeled and
chopped
4 tsp paprika, plus extra to dust
1.1 litres (2 pints) vegetable stock

450ml (¾ pint) milk
4 tbsp double cream
75g (3oz) sliced chorizo sausage,
cut into fine strips
salt and ground black pepper
parsnip crisps and freshly grated
Parmesan to serve

Melt the butter in a large heavy-based pan over a gentle heat. Add the onion and cook for 5 minutes until soft. Mix in the potatoes, parsnips and paprika. Cook gently, stirring occasionally, for 15 minutes or until the vegetables begin to soften.

Add the stock, milk and cream and season with salt and pepper. Bring to the boil, then reduce the heat and simmer for 25 minutes or until the vegetables are very soft. Add 50g (2oz) chorizo. Leave the soup to cool a little, then whiz in batches in a blender or food processor until smooth. The soup can be thinned with additional stock or milk, if liked. Check the seasoning and put back into the pan.

Reheat the soup gently. Ladle into warmed bowls, top each with parsnip crisps, sprinkle with the remaining chorizo and a little Parmesan and dust with paprika.

Freezing Tip
To freeze: Complete the recipe to the end of step 2, then cool, pack and freeze for up to one month.
To use: Thaw the soup overnight at cool room temperature and then complete the recipe as above.

Sweet Potato Soup

serves 8

1 tbsp olive oil
1 large onion, finely chopped
2 tsp coriander seeds, crushed
2 fresh red chillies, seeded and
   chopped (see Cook's Tip)
1 butternut squash, about 750g
   (1lb 10oz), peeled and chopped

2 sweet potatoes, peeled and roughly
   chopped
2 tomatoes, skinned and diced
1.7 litres (3 pints) hot vegetable stock
cheese straws to serve

Heat the oil in a large saucepan over a gentle heat and fry the onion for about
10 minutes until soft. Add the coriander seeds and chillies to the pan and cook
for a further 1–2 minutes.

Add the squash, sweet potatoes and tomatoes and cook for 5 minutes. Add the
hot stock, cover and bring to the boil, then reduce the heat and simmer gently
for 15 minutes or until the vegetables are soft. Leave the soup to cool a little,
then whiz in batches in a blender or food processor until smooth. Reheat gently
and serve with a sprinkling of black pepper and cheese straws.

Freezing Tip
To freeze: Complete the recipe, then cool, pack and freeze for up to 3 months.
To use: Thaw the soup for 4 hours at cool room temperature. Put in a pan, bring
to the boil and simmer for 10 minutes.

Cook's Tips
Chillies vary enormously in strength, from quite mild to blisteringly hot, depending
on their type and ripeness. Taste a small piece first to check it's not too hot for
you. Be extremely careful when handling chillies not to touch or rub your eyes
with your fingers, as they will sting. Wash knives immediately after handling them
for the same reason. As a precaution, use rubber gloves when preparing them.

Leek and Potato Soup

serves 4

25g (1oz) butter
1 onion, finely chopped
1 garlic clove, crushed
550g (1¼lb) leeks, trimmed and
    chopped

200g (7oz) floury potatoes, peeled
    and sliced
1.3 litres (2¼ pints) hot vegetable stock
crème fraîche and chopped chives
    to garnish

Melt the butter in a pan over a gentle heat. Cook the onion for 10–15 minutes until soft. Add the garlic and cook for 1 minute. Add the leeks and cook for 5–10 minutes until softened. Add the potatoes and toss together with the leeks.

Pour in the hot stock and bring to the boil, then reduce the heat and simmer the soup for 20 minutes until the potatoes are tender.

Leave the soup to cool a little, then whiz in batches in a blender or food processor until smooth.

To serve, reheat the soup gently. Ladle into warmed bowls and garnish with crème fraîche and some snipped chives.

Roasted Tomato and Pepper Soup

serves
6

1.4kg (3lb) full-flavoured tomatoes,
preferably vine-ripened
2 red peppers, cored, seeded and
chopped
4 garlic cloves, crushed
3 small onions, thinly sliced

20g (¾oz) fresh thyme sprigs
4 tbsp olive oil
4 tbsp Worcestershire sauce
4 tbsp vodka
salt and ground black pepper
6 tbsp double cream to serve

Preheat the oven to 200°C (180°C fan oven) mark 6. Put the tomatoes into a large roasting tin with the peppers, garlic and onions. Scatter 6 thyme sprigs over the top, drizzle with oil and roast in the oven for 25 minutes. Turn the vegetables over and roast for a further 30–40 minutes until tender and slightly charred.

Put one-third of the vegetables into a blender or food processor with 300ml (½ pint) boiled water. Add the Worcestershire sauce and vodka and season with salt and pepper. Whiz until smooth, then pass through a sieve into a saucepan.

Whiz the remaining vegetables with 450ml (¾ pint) boiled water, then sieve and add to the pan.

To serve, warm the soup thoroughly, stirring occasionally. Ladle into warmed bowls, add 1 tbsp double cream to each bowl, then drag a cocktail stick through the cream to swirl it. Sprinkle with fresh thyme leaves and serve immediately.

Carrot and Coriander Soup

serves 6

40g (1½ oz) butter
175g (6oz) leeks, trimmed and sliced
450g (1lb) carrots, sliced
2 tsp ground coriander
1 tsp plain flour

1.1 litres (2 pints) vegetable stock
150ml (¼ pint) single cream
salt and ground black pepper
coriander leaves, roughly torn, to serve

Melt the butter in a large pan. Add the leeks and carrots, stir, then cover and cook gently for 7–10 minutes until the vegetables begin to soften but not colour.

Stir in the ground coriander and flour and cook, stirring, for 1 minute.

Add the stock and bring to the boil, stirring. Season with salt and pepper, then reduce the heat, cover the pan and simmer gently for about 20 minutes, until the vegetables are tender.

Leave the soup to cool a little, then whiz in batches in a blender or food processor until quite smooth. Return the soup to the pan and stir in the cream. Adjust the seasoning and reheat gently; do not boil.

Ladle the soup into warmed bowls, scatter with torn coriander leaves and serve.

Mixed Mushroom Soup

serves 4

15g (½ oz) dried porcini mushrooms
1 tbsp sunflower oil, plus 50ml (2fl oz)
  to shallow-fry
1 small onion, chopped
450g (1lb) chestnut mushrooms,
  chopped
600ml (1 pint) hot vegetable stock

2 slices white bread, crusts removed,
  cut into cubes
2 garlic cloves, finely sliced
salt and ground black pepper
freshly chopped flat-leafed parsley
  to garnish

Put the porcini into a bowl, pour 75ml (2½fl oz) boiling water over them and leave to soak for 10 minutes. Strain the porcini, put the liquid to one side, then chop roughly, keeping 1 tbsp for a garnish.

Heat 1 tbsp oil in a pan. Add the onion and porcini and cook over a medium heat for 5 minutes. Add the chestnut mushrooms, increase the heat and brown lightly for 5 minutes. Add the reserved porcini liquid and the stock, and bring to the boil. Season well with salt and pepper, reduce the heat and simmer for 20 minutes.

To make croûtons, heat 50ml (2fl oz) oil in a frying pan. Add the bread and garlic and stir-fry for 2 minutes until golden. Drain on kitchen paper.

Take the soup off the heat and leave to cool a little. Whiz in a blender or food processor until smooth, then transfer to a clean pan. Reheat gently, then ladle into warmed bowls and serve topped with the croûtons, reserved porcini and a sprinkling of parsley.

Courgette and Leek Soup

serves
8

1 tbsp olive oil
1 onion, finely chopped
2 leeks, trimmed and sliced
900g (2lb) courgettes, grated
1.6 litres (2¾ pints) hot vegetable
   or chicken stock

4 short rosemary sprigs
1 small baguette
125g (4oz) grated Gruyère cheese
salt and ground black pepper

Heat the oil in a large pan. Add the onion and leeks and cook for 5–10 minutes. Add the courgettes and cook, stirring, for a further 5 minutes.

Add the hot stock and 3 rosemary sprigs, then bring to the boil. Season with salt and pepper, reduce the heat and simmer for 20 minutes.

Preheat the grill to medium-high. Slice the bread diagonally into eight and grill for 1–2 minutes on one side until golden. Turn the bread over, sprinkle with the cheese and season. Grill for a further 1–2 minutes. Keep the croûtes warm.

Leave the soup to cool a little. Remove the rosemary stalks and whiz in batches in a blender or food processor until smooth. Pour into a clean pan and reheat gently.

Ladle into warmed soup bowls, garnish with the croûtes and sprinkle with the remaining rosemary leaves.

Cream of Jerusalem Artichoke Soup

serves 6

450g (1lb) Jerusalem artichokes
50g (2oz) butter
2 shallots, diced
1 tsp mild curry paste
900ml (1½ pints) vegetable stock
150ml (¼ pint) single cream

freshly grated nutmeg to taste
pinch of cayenne pepper
4 tbsp freshly grated Parmesan
salt and ground black pepper
3–4 slices hot Melba toast to serve
    (see Cook's Tips)

Scrub the Jerusalem artichokes thoroughly, pat dry, and then slice thinly.

Melt the butter in a large pan, add the shallots and cook gently for 10 minutes until soft and golden.

Stir in the curry paste and cook for 1 minute. Add the sliced artichokes and stock and stir well, then bring to the boil. Reduce the heat, cover the pan and simmer for about 15 minutes until the artichokes are tender.

Add the cream, nutmeg and cayenne to the soup. Transfer to a blender or food processor and whiz until smooth, then pass through a sieve into a clean pan.

Reheat the soup gently and stir in the grated Parmesan. Taste and adjust the seasoning. Ladle into warmed bowls and serve at once, with the Melba toast.

Cook's Tips

Melba Toast: Cut 4–5 thin slices from a day-old loaf of wholemeal bread and toast lightly on both sides. Quickly cut off the crusts and split each slice in two horizontally. Bake in a 180°C (160°C fan) mark 4 oven for 10–15 minutes until crisp and curled.

For a less rich soup: Use semi-skimmed milk rather than single cream.

Easy Pea Soup

serves
4

1 small baguette, thinly sliced
2 tbsp basil-infused olive oil, plus extra
    to drizzle

450g (1lb) frozen peas, thawed
600ml (1 pint) vegetable stock
salt and ground black pepper

Preheat the oven to 220°C (200°C fan oven) mark 7. To make the croûtons, put the bread on a baking sheet, drizzle with 2 tbsp olive oil and then bake in the oven for 10–15 minutes until golden.

Meanwhile, put the peas in a food processor, add the stock and season with salt and pepper. Whiz for 2–3 minutes.

Pour the soup into a pan and bring to the boil, then reduce the heat and simmer for 10 minutes. Spoon into warmed bowls, add the croûtons, drizzle with extra oil and sprinkle with salt and pepper. Serve immediately.

Cook's Tip
Serve this smooth, rich soup with warmed bridge rolls, before a main course of plain roast or grilled meat.

Turkey and Chestnut Soup

serves
4

25g (1oz) butter or margarine
1 large onion, chopped
225g (8oz) Brussels sprouts
900ml (1½ pints) turkey stock made
    from leftover carcass and any
    leftover turkey meat

400g can whole chestnuts, drained
2 tsp freshly chopped thyme
    or 1 tsp dried thyme
salt and ground black pepper
stock or milk to finish
thyme sprigs to garnish

Melt the fat in a large heavy-based saucepan, add the onion and fry gently for 5 minutes until it has softened.

Trim the sprouts and cut a cross in the base of each one. Add to the onion, cover the pan with a lid and cook gently for 5 minutes, shaking the pan frequently.

Pour in the stock and bring to the boil, then add the remaining ingredients, with salt and pepper to taste. Reduce the heat, cover the pan and simmer for 30 minutes until the vegetables are tender.

Leave the soup to cool a little, then whiz in batches in a blender or food processor until smooth. Return to the rinsed-out pan and reheat gently, then thin down with either stock or milk, according to taste.

Taste and adjust the seasoning. To serve, ladle the soup into warmed bowls and garnish with sprigs of thyme.

Cook's Tip
Serve this soup for an informal family lunch with hot garlic bread, wholemeal toast, cheese on toast or hot sausage rolls.

Broccoli and Goat's Cheese Soup

serves
6

50g (2oz) butter
2 medium onions, chopped
1 litre (1¾ pints) vegetable, chicken
   or turkey stock
700g (1½lb) broccoli, broken into
   florets, stout stalks peeled and
   chopped

1 head of garlic, unpeeled and
   separated into cloves
1 tbsp olive oil
150g (5oz) goat's cheese
salt and ground black pepper

Preheat the oven to 200°C (180°C fan oven) mark 6. Melt the butter in a pan over a gentle heat. Add the onions, then cover the pan and cook for 4–5 minutes until translucent. Add half the stock and bring to the boil. Add the broccoli and return to the boil, then cover the pan, reduce the heat and simmer gently for 15–20 minutes or until the broccoli is tender.

Toss the cloves of garlic in the oil and tip into a roasting tin. Roast in the oven for 15 minutes until soft when squeezed.

Leave the soup to cool a little, then add the goat's cheese and whiz in batches in a blender or food processor until smooth. Return the soup to the pan and add the remaining stock. Reheat gently and season to taste with salt and pepper.

Ladle the soup into warmed bowls, squeeze the garlic out of their skins and scatter over the soup, add a sprinkling of black pepper and serve.

Try Something Different
Double the quantity of goat's cheese if you prefer a stronger taste. Or instead of goat's cheese, try substituting a soft garlic cheese for a really garlicky flavour.

Cream of Chicken Soup

serves 4

3 tbsp plain flour
150ml (¼ pint) milk
1.1 litres (2 pints) homemade chicken
   stock
125g (4oz) cooked chicken, diced

1 tsp lemon juice
a pinch of freshly grated nutmeg
2 tbsp single cream
salt and ground black pepper
croûtons and parsley sprigs to garnish

Put the flour into a large bowl, add a little of the milk and blend until it makes a smooth cream.

Bring the stock to the boil, then stir it into the blended mixture. Return to the pan and simmer gently for 20 minutes.

Stir in the chicken, lemon juice and nutmeg. Season to taste with salt and pepper. Mix the rest of the milk with the cream and stir in, then reheat without boiling.

Taste and adjust the seasoning. Ladle the soup into warmed bowls, sprinkle with croûtons and parsley sprigs and serve.

Cook's Tip
Serve this smooth, rich soup with warmed bridge rolls, before a main course of plain roast or grilled meat.

Creamy Watercress Soup

serves
6

250g (9oz) watercress
50g (2oz) butter
1 onion, finely chopped
700g (1½lb) potatoes, peeled
   and cut into small pieces
900ml (1½ pints) milk

900ml (1½ pints) vegetable stock
6 tbsp single cream
salt and ground black pepper
Parmesan Crisps (see Cook's Tip)
   to serve (optional)

Trim the watercress and discard any coarse stalks. Reserve a few sprigs of the watercress to garnish the soup, then roughly chop the rest.

Melt the butter in a large pan, add the onion and cook gently for 8–10 minutes until soft. Add the potatoes and cook for 1 minute. Pour in the milk and stock and bring to the boil. Reduce the heat and simmer for 15–20 minutes until tender.

Remove from the heat. Stir in the chopped watercress, then transfer to a blender and blend, in batches, until smooth. Pour the soup into a clean pan, then add the cream and season with salt and pepper. Heat through, and serve garnished with the reserved watercress sprigs, with the Parmesan crisps on the side.

Cook's Tip

To make the Parmesan crisps, preheat the oven to 200°C (180°C fan oven) mark 6 and line 2 baking sheets with baking parchment. Put heaped tablespoons of Parmesan on the sheets, spacing them well apart, and spread each one out. Sprinkle with poppy seeds and bake for 5–10 minutes until lacy golden. Leave on the sheets for 2–3 minutes to firm up slightly, then transfer to a wire rack to cool.

Beetroot Soup

serves 4

1 tbsp olive oil
1 onion, finely chopped
750g (1lb 10oz) raw beetroot,
    peeled and cut into 1cm (½in)
    cubes
275g (10oz) potatoes, peeled and
    roughly chopped

2 litres (3½ pints) hot vegetable stock
juice of 1 lemon
4 tbsp soured cream
25g (1oz) mixed root vegetable crisps
salt and ground black pepper
2 tbsp chopped chives to garnish

Heat the oil in a large pan, add the onion and cook for 5 minutes. Add the vegetables and cook for a further 5 minutes.

Add the hot stock and lemon juice, then bring to the boil. Season with salt and pepper, reduce the heat and simmer, half-covered, for 25 minutes. Leave to cool a little, then whiz in batches in a blender or food processor until smooth.

Cool half the soup, then freeze it. Pour the remainder into a clean pan and reheat gently. Ladle into warmed bowls, add 1 tbsp soured cream to each bowl, top with a few vegetable crisps and sprinkle the chopped chives on top to serve.

Freezing Tip
To freeze: Complete the recipe to the end of step 2, then cool half or all the soup, pack and freeze for up to three months.
To use: Thaw the soup overnight at cool room temperature. Reheat gently and simmer over a low heat for 5 minutes.

Creamed Celeriac and Parmesan Soup

serves
4

2 tbsp sunflower oil
175g (6oz) onions, roughly chopped
1 garlic clove, crushed
450g (1lb) each celeriac and potatoes,
    peeled and roughly chopped
1.1 litres (2 pints) vegetable stock
1 bouquet garni (see page 59)

600ml (1 pint) full-fat milk
284ml carton double cream
1 tbsp lemon juice
8 tbsp freshly grated Parmesan
Toasted Parmesan to serve
    (see Cook's Tip)

Heat the oil in a large saucepan, then add the onions and garlic. Cook slowly for
4–5 minutes or until golden brown.

Add the celeriac, potatoes, stock and bouquet garni and bring to the boil, then
reduce the heat and simmer gently for about 20–25 minutes or until the celeriac
and potatoes are tender.

Leave the soup to cool a little, then discard the bouquet garni. Whiz the soup
in batches in a blender or food processor until smooth. Pour into a clean pan,
add the milk, cream and lemon juice and season to taste with salt and pepper.
Simmer for a further 10 minutes.

To serve, put 1 tbsp grated Parmesan in the bottom of each warmed serving
bowl. Ladle in the soup, grind over some black pepper and garnish with the
Toasted Parmesan (see below).

Cook's Tip
Toasted Parmesan: Sprinkle 25g (1oz) finely grated Parmesan on to a baking
sheet. Put under a hot grill until melted and golden. Cool, then crumble and
store in an airtight container for up to one week.

Pumpkin and Butternut Squash Soup

serves
4

900g (2lb) pumpkin, peeled and
   roughly diced
750g (1lb 10oz) butternut squash,
   peeled and roughly diced
125g (4oz) shallots, roughly chopped
1 fat garlic clove, chopped
1 tsp coriander seeds, crushed
125g (4oz) butter, melted

600ml (1 pint) vegetable stock
600ml (1 pint) full-fat milk
salt and ground black pepper
basil sprigs and soured cream to
   garnish
crusty bread or small Yorkshire
   puddings to serve

Preheat the oven to 220°C (200°C fan oven) mark 7. Put the pumpkin, butternut squash, shallots, garlic and coriander seeds into a large roasting tin and toss with the melted butter. Season the vegetables well with salt and pepper and bake for about 30 minutes until golden and just cooked through.

Meanwhile, in separate pans, heat the stock and the milk.

Transfer the vegetables to a large pan, then pour the hot stock into the roasting tin and stir to loosen the remaining bits in the tin. Add this to the vegetables in the pan, then stir in the milk.

Put three-quarters of the soup into a blender or food processor and whiz until smooth. Mash the remaining soup mixture, then stir the two together and reheat gently. Ladle into warmed bowls, garnish with basil and swirls of soured cream, then serve with crusty bread or small Yorkshire puddings.

Kale and Leek Soup

serves
6

450g (1lb) leeks, trimmed
25g (1oz) butter
2 rashers streaky bacon, rinded and
    chopped
450g (1lb) kale, washed and chopped
900ml (1½ pints) chicken stock

2 tbsp freshly chopped parsley
½ tsp freshly chopped tarragon
2 tbsp cornflour
150ml (¼ pint) milk
salt and ground black pepper

Slice the leeks, place in a colander or sieve and wash thoroughly. Drain.

Melt the butter in a saucepan, then add the leeks and bacon and cook gently for 5 minutes. Remove from the pan and set aside. Add the kale to the pan and cook for 5 minutes.

Return the leeks and bacon to the pan with the stock and herbs and season to taste with salt and pepper. Cover the pan and bring to the boil, then reduce the heat and simmer gently for 35–40 minutes.

Leave the soup to cool a little, then whiz in batches in a blender or food processor until smooth.

Return the soup to a clean pan. Blend the cornflour to a smooth paste with the milk. Add to the pan, reheat gently until hot, stirring, and cook for 2 minutes. Ladle into warmed bowls and serve.

Meal in a bowl

Fast Fish Soup

serves 4

1 leek, trimmed and finely chopped
4 fat garlic cloves, crushed
3 celery sticks, finely chopped
1 small fennel bulb, finely chopped
1 red chilli, seeded and finely chopped
3 tbsp olive oil
50ml (2fl oz) dry white wine
about 750g (1lb 11oz) mixed fish and
    shellfish, such as haddock and

monkfish fillets, peeled and
deveined raw prawns, and fresh
mussels, scrubbed and cleaned
(discard any mussels that don't
close when tapped on a worksurface
or that have broken shells)
4 tomatoes, chopped
20g (¾ oz) freshly chopped thyme
salt and ground black pepper

Put the leek into a large saucepan and add the garlic, celery, fennel, chilli and oil. Cook over a medium heat for 5 minutes or until the vegetables are soft and beginning to colour.

Stir in 1.1 litres (2 pints) boiling water and the wine. Bring to the boil, then reduce the heat, cover the pan and simmer for 5 minutes.

Cut the white fish into large chunks. Add to the soup with the tomatoes and thyme. Continue to simmer gently until the fish turns opaque. Add the prawns, simmer for 1 minute, then add the mussels, if you're using them.

As soon as all the mussels have opened (discard any that do not), season the soup with salt and pepper. Ladle into warmed bowls and serve immediately.

Try Something Different
To give the soup more of a kick, stir in 2 tbsp Pernod instead of the wine. Garlic croûtes are traditionally served with fish soup; they can be made while the soup is simmering. Toast small slices of baguette, spread with garlic mayonnaise and sprinkle with grated cheese. Float in the hot soup just before serving.

Navarin of Cod Soup

serves 6

175g (6oz) podded broad beans
25g (1oz) butter
2 tbsp sunflower oil
1 onion, sliced
225g (8oz) baby carrots, trimmed
    and halved
225g (8oz) courgettes, cut into
    2cm (¾in) chunks
1 garlic clove, crushed
1.1kg (2½lb) thick cod fillet, skinned

4 tbsp plain flour
150ml (¼ pint) dry white wine
300ml (½ pint) fish stock
1 tbsp lemon juice
3 tbsp double cream
2 tbsp freshly chopped flat-leafed
    parsley
salt and ground black pepper
baby new potatoes to serve (optional)

If the beans are large, blanch them in boiling water for 1–2 minutes, then drain and refresh in cold water.

Heat half the butter and half the oil in a large sauté pan. Add the onion, carrots, courgettes and garlic and cook gently until softened and just beginning to brown. Remove from the pan and put to one side.

Season the fish with salt and pepper, then dust lightly with the flour. Heat the remaining butter and oil in the pan, add the fish and brown on all sides. Remove from the pan and put to one side.

Add the wine to the pan, scraping up any sediment from the bottom. Simmer for 1–2 minutes, then put the carrot mixture and fish back in the pan. Add the beans and stock. Bring to a simmer, cover and simmer gently for about 10 minutes until the fish is opaque and flakes easily. Stir in the lemon juice, cream and parsley. Ladle into warmed bowls and serve with baby new potatoes, if you like.

Smoked Cod and Sweetcorn Chowder

serves 6

130g pack cubed pancetta
50g (2oz) butter
3 leeks, about 450g (1lb), trimmed
    and thinly sliced
25g (1oz) plain flour
600ml (1 pint) semi-skimmed or
    full-fat milk
700g (1½lb) undyed smoked cod loin
    or haddock, skinned and cut into
    2cm (¾in) cubes

326g can sweetcorn in water, drained
450g (1lb) small new potatoes,
    scrubbed and sliced
150ml (¼ pint) double cream
½ tsp paprika
salt and ground black pepper
2 tbsp freshly chopped flat-leafed
    parsley to garnish

Fry the pancetta in a large pan over a gentle heat until the fat runs out. Add the butter to the pan to melt, then add the leeks and cook until softened.

Stir in the flour and cook for a few seconds, then pour in the milk and 300ml (½ pint) cold water. Add the fish to the pan with the sweetcorn and potatoes. Bring to the boil, then reduce the heat and simmer for 10–15 minutes until the potatoes are cooked.

Stir in the cream, season to taste with salt and pepper and the paprika and cook for 2–3 minutes to warm through. Ladle into warmed shallow bowls and sprinkle each one with a little chopped parsley. Serve immediately.

Squash, Lentil and Prawn Soup

serves 6

75g (3oz) butter
75g (3oz) each carrots, onions, celery
    and leeks, roughly chopped
2 garlic cloves, crushed
175g (6oz) Puy lentils
900ml (1½ pints) fish stock
200ml (7fl oz) vermouth
140ml (4½ fl oz) double cream

2 fresh thyme sprigs
2 bay leaves
6–8 small squashes, each weighing
    about 700g (1lb 9oz)
18–24 large raw prawns, peeled
    and deveined
salt and ground black pepper
chopped chives to garnish

Heat 50g (2oz) butter in a large saucepan and cook the vegetables, stirring occasionally, for 5 minutes. Add the garlic and cook for 1 minute. Stir in the lentils, stock and 150ml (¼ pint) vermouth with the cream, herbs and seasoning. Add 300ml (½ pint) water. Bring to the boil, then cover the pan and simmer for 40–45 minutes until the vegetables are tender. Discard the herbs.

Meanwhile, preheat the oven to 200°C (180°C fan oven) mark 6. Trim the bases of the squashes so that they are flat, and cut the tops off at the stalk end. Scoop out the seeds. Put the squashes in a roasting tin and cook for 40 minutes or until tender. Scoop out some of the flesh and add to the soup. Leave the soup to cool a little, then whiz in batches in a blender or food processor until smooth. Pass through a fine sieve, if you like, and adjust the seasoning. If the soup is too thick, dilute with stock or water, put back into the wiped-out pan and keep warm.

Put the prawns into a pan with the remaining butter and vermouth and simmer for 2–3 minutes until the prawns turn pink. Strain the prawn liquid into the soup. Ladle into warmed bowls or the hollowed-out squashes, add the prawns and garnish with the chives.

Freezing Tip
To freeze: Complete the soup to the end of step 2, then cool quickly, pack and freeze for up to one month.
To use: Thaw the soup overnight at cool room temperature, then complete the recipe as above.

French Onion Soup

serves 4

75g (3oz) butter
700g (1½lb) small onions, finely
  chopped
3 garlic cloves, crushed
1 tbsp plain flour
200ml (7fl oz) dry white wine
1.5 litres (2½ pints) vegetable stock

1 bouquet garni (see Cook's Tip)
salt and ground black pepper
1 small baguette, cut into slices 1cm
  (½in) thick, to serve
50g (2oz) Gruyère cheese or Cheddar,
  grated, to serve

Melt the butter in a large heavy-based pan. Add the onions and cook slowly over a very low heat, stirring frequently, until very soft and golden brown; this should take at least 30 minutes. Add the garlic and flour and cook, stirring, for 1 minute. Pour in the wine and let bubble until reduced by half. Add the stock, bouquet garni and seasoning. Bring to the boil, then reduce the heat and simmer gently, uncovered, for 20–30 minutes.

Discard the bouquet garni. Let the soup cool a little. Put one-third into a blender or food processor, whiz until smooth, then stir back into the soup in the pan.

Preheat the grill. Lightly toast the slices of French bread on both sides. Reheat the soup and adjust the seasoning. Divide the soup among four ovenproof soup bowls. Float two or three slices of toast on each portion and sprinkle thickly with the grated cheese. Stand the bowls under the hot grill until the cheese has melted and turned golden brown. Serve at once.

Cook's Tip
To make a bouquet garni, tie together a sprig each of thyme and parsley with a bay leaf and a piece of celery.

Quick Winter Minestrone

serves 4

2 tbsp olive oil
1 small onion, finely chopped
1 carrot, chopped
1 celery stick, chopped
1 garlic clove, crushed
2 tbsp freshly chopped thyme
1 litre (1¾ pints) vegetable stock
400g can chopped tomatoes

400g can borlotti beans, drained and
   rinsed
125g (4oz) minestrone pasta
175g (6oz) Savoy cabbage, shredded
salt and ground black pepper
fresh ready-made pesto (see page 105),
   toasted ciabatta and extra virgin
   olive oil to serve

Heat the olive oil in a large pan and add the onion, carrot and celery. Cook for 8–10 minutes until softened, then add the garlic and thyme. Fry for 2–3 minutes.

Add the stock, tomatoes and half the borlotti beans. Mash the remaining beans, stir into the soup and simmer for 30 minutes, adding the minestrone pasta and cabbage for the last 10 minutes of cooking time.

Check the seasoning and correct, if necessary. Ladle into warmed bowls and serve with a dollop of fresh pesto on top and slices of toasted ciabatta drizzled with extra virgin olive oil on the side.

Turkey, Ham and Spinach Broth

125g (4oz) green or yellow split peas, soaked overnight in double their volume of cold water
25g (1oz) butter
225g (8oz) onions, chopped
1 tbsp ground coriander
40g (1½oz) pearl barley
2 litres (3½ pints) ham or turkey stock
1 bouquet garni
225g (8oz) potatoes, peeled and cut into chunks

400g (14oz) carrots, cut into chunks
150g (5oz) each cooked turkey and ham, cut into chunks
150g (5oz) baby spinach leaves
salt and ground black pepper
coriander sprigs and black pepper to garnish
50g (2oz) finely grated Parmesan to serve (optional)

Drain the split peas, put into a pan and cover with cold water. Bring to the boil, reduce the heat and simmer for 10 minutes. Drain the peas and discard the liquid.

Meanwhile, melt the butter in a pan, add the onions and cook for 5 minutes or until soft but not coloured. Add the ground coriander and cook for 30 seconds.

Add the split peas, pearl barley and stock. Tie the bay leaf, celery and thyme sprig together and add to the pan. Bring to the boil, then reduce the heat and simmer for 40 minutes or until the peas and barley are tender. Add the potatoes and cook for 5 minutes, then add the carrots and cook for 5–10 minutes. Season to taste with salt and pepper.

Add the turkey, ham and spinach to the pan and bring back to the boil, then reduce the heat and simmer for 2–3 minutes. Ladle into warmed bowls, garnish with coriander sprigs and pepper and serve with grated Parmesan, if you like.

Scotch Broth

1 piece of marrow bone, about
350g (12oz)
1.4kg (3lb) piece of beef skirt
(ask your butcher for this)
300ml (½ pint) broth mix (to include
pearl barley, red lentils, split peas
and green peas), soaked according
to the packet instructions

2 carrots, finely chopped
1 parsnip, finely chopped
2 onions, finely chopped
¼ white cabbage, finely chopped
1 leek, trimmed and finely chopped
½ tbsp salt
ground black pepper
2 tbsp freshly chopped parsley to serve

Put the marrow bone and beef skirt into a 5.7 litre (10 pint) stock pot and add
2.6 litres (4½ pints) cold water – there should be enough to cover the meat.

Bring the water to the boil. Remove any scum from the surface with a spoon and
discard. Reduce the heat to low, add the broth mix and simmer, partially covered,
for 1½ hours, skimming the surface occasionally.

Add the carrots, parsnip, onions, cabbage, leek and another 600ml (1 pint) cold
water. Cover to bring to the boil quickly, then reduce the heat and simmer for
30 minutes.

Remove the marrow bone and piece of beef from the broth. Add a few shreds of
beef to the broth if you like. Season the broth well with the salt and some pepper
and stir in the chopped parsley. Ladle into warmed bowls and serve hot.

Cook's Tip
This is really two meals in one: a starter and a main course. The beef flavours
the stock and is removed before serving. Later you divide up the meat and serve
it with mashed potatoes, swedes or turnips.

Split Pea and Ham Soup

serves
6

500g pack dried yellow split peas,
    soaked overnight (see Cook's Tip)
25g (1oz) butter
1 large onion, finely chopped
125g (4oz) rindless smoked streaky
    bacon rashers, roughly chopped
1 garlic clove, crushed

1.7 litres (3 pints) well-flavoured ham
    or vegetable stock
1 bouquet garni
1 tsp dried oregano
salt and ground black pepper
125g (4oz) cooked ham, chopped
cracked black pepper to serve

Drain the soaked split peas. Melt the butter in a large pan, add the onion, bacon and garlic and cook over a low heat for about 10 minutes until the onion is soft.

Add the drained split peas to the pan with the stock. Bring to the boil and skim the surface. Add the bouquet garni and oregano, then season with salt and pepper. Reduce the heat, cover the pan and simmer for 45 minutes to 1 hour or until the peas are very soft.

Cool a little, then whiz half the soup in a blender or food processor until smooth. Return to the saucepan and reheat, then add the ham and check the seasoning. Ladle into warmed bowls and sprinkle with cracked black pepper to serve.

Cook's Tip

Dried peas form the base of this comforting soup. First, you need to soak them overnight in about 1 litre (1¾ pints) cold water. If you forget, put them straight into a pan with the water, bring to the boil and cook for 1–2 minutes, then leave to stand for 2 hours before using.

Autumn Vegetable Soup

serves
4

50g (2oz) butter
1 medium onion, diced
450g (1lb) potatoes, peeled and diced
100g (3½oz) diced bacon
1 garlic clove, chopped
100g (3½oz) white of leek, chopped
2 Cox Orange Pippins apples,
   unpeeled, cored and chopped

2 tsp dried thyme
1 tsp dill seeds (optional)
salt and ground black pepper
600ml (1 pint) dry cider
900ml (1½ pints) hot vegetable stock
125g (4oz) Savoy cabbage leaves,
   shredded

Melt the butter in a large saucepan, then add the onion, potatoes, bacon, garlic, leek, apple, thyme and dill, if using. Season to taste with salt and pepper, stir, then cover the pan and cook gently for 15 minutes.

Add the cider and bring to the boil, then reduce the heat and simmer gently for 5 minutes. Add the hot stock to the pan and simmer for about 15 minutes until the potatoes are soft.

Pour half the soup into a blender or food processor and whiz until smooth, then add to the remaining soup in the pan. Reheat gently, add the shredded cabbage and simmer for a further 3 minutes. Ladle into warmed bowls and serve.

Cock-a-Leekie Soup

1 oven-ready chicken, about
   1.4kg (3lb)
2 onions, roughly chopped
2 carrots, roughly chopped
2 celery sticks, roughly chopped
1 bay leaf
25g (1oz) butter
900g (2lb) leeks, trimmed and sliced
125g (4oz) ready-to-eat stoned prunes,
   sliced

salt and ground black pepper
freshly chopped parsley to serve

For the dumplings
125g (4oz) self-raising white flour
a pinch of salt
50g (2oz) shredded suet
2 tbsp freshly chopped parsley
2 tbsp freshly chopped thyme

Put the chicken into a saucepan in which it fits quite snugly. Add the chopped vegetables, bay leaf and chicken giblets (if available). Add 1.7 litres (3 pints) water and bring to the boil, then reduce the heat, cover the pan and leave to simmer gently for 1 hour.

Meanwhile, melt the butter in another large saucepan, add the leeks and fry gently for 10 minutes or until softened.

Remove the chicken from the pan, then strain the stock and set aside. Strip the chicken from the bones and shred roughly. Add to the stock with the prunes and softened leeks.

To make the dumplings, sift the flour and salt into a bowl. Stir in the suet, herbs and about 5 tbsp water to make a fairly firm dough. Lightly shape the dough into 2.5cm (1in) balls. Bring the soup just to the boil and season well. Reduce the heat, add the dumplings and cover the pan with a lid. Simmer for 15–20 minutes until the dumplings are light and fluffy. Serve scattered with chopped parsley.

Chicken and Mushroom Broth

serves 4

4 skinless chicken breasts
pesto (see Cook's Tip), made omitting
   the Parmesan
1.1 litres (2 pints) chicken stock
100ml (3½fl oz) medium sherry
150g (5oz) exotic mushrooms, cleaned
   and sliced

1 red chilli, seeded and halved
75g (3oz) conchigliette pasta
2 tbsp soy sauce
a small handful of chopped pak choi
   or spinach leaves
a dash of Tabasco to serve (optional)

Preheat the oven to 200°C (180°C fan oven) mark 6. Make a few slashes in the chicken breasts, then rub the pesto over the chicken, pushing it into the cuts. Put into a roasting tin and roast for 20 minutes.

Meanwhile, put the stock into a pan with the sherry and bring to the boil.

Add the mushrooms, chilli and pasta. Cover the pan and simmer for 3 minutes until the pasta is cooked. Stir in the soy sauce.

Slice the chicken into the broth with the pak choi or spinach.

Ladle the soup into warmed bowls and serve immediately. Add a dash of Tabasco if you like it hot!

Cook's Tip
Pesto: Put a 20g pack roughly chopped basil into a food processor. Add 25g (1oz) finely grated Parmesan, 50g (2oz) pinenuts and 4 tbsp extra virgin olive oil and whiz to a rough paste. Alternatively, grind in a pestle and mortar. Season with salt and plenty of ground black pepper.

Pasta and Chickpea Soup with Pesto

serves
6

3 tbsp olive oil

1 onion, chopped

2 garlic cloves, finely chopped

1 small leek, trimmed and sliced

1 tsp freshly chopped rosemary

400g can chickpeas

1.2 litres (2 pints) vegetable stock

4 ripe tomatoes, skinned and chopped

1 courgette, diced

125g (4oz) shelled peas

125g (4oz) French beans, halved

125g (4oz) shelled broad beans

50g (2oz) dried pastina (small soup
   pasta)

2 tbsp freshly chopped parsley

salt and ground black pepper

pesto (see page 105) and freshly grated
pecorino or Parmesan to serve

Heat the oil in a large saucepan, add the onion, garlic, leek and rosemary and fry gently for 5–6 minutes or until softened but not coloured. Add the chickpeas with their liquid, the stock and tomatoes. Bring to the boil, then reduce the heat, cover the pan and simmer for 40 minutes.

Add the courgette, peas, French beans and broad beans to the pan. Return to the boil, then reduce the heat and simmer for 10 minutes. Add the pasta and parsley and simmer for 6–8 minutes until al dente. Season to taste with salt and pepper.

Ladle the soup into warmed bowls and serve topped with a spoonful of pesto and a sprinkling of cheese.

Pepper and Lentil Soup

serves 6

1 tbsp oil
1 medium onion, finely chopped
1 celery stick, chopped
1 leek, trimmed and chopped
1 carrot, chopped
2 red peppers, seeded and diced
225g (8oz) red lentils

400g can chopped tomatoes
1 litre (1¾ pints) hot light vegetable
    stock
25g pack flat-leafed parsley, chopped
salt and ground black pepper
toast to serve

Heat the oil in a saucepan. Add the onion, celery, leek and carrot and cook for 10–15 minutes until soft.

Add the red peppers and cook for 5 minutes. Stir in the red lentils, add the tomatoes and hot stock and season to taste with salt and pepper.

Cover the pan and bring to the boil, then reduce the heat and cook, uncovered, for 25 minutes until the lentils are soft and the vegetables are tender.

Stir in the parsley. Ladle the soup into warmed bowls and serve with toast.

Hot and spicy

Cauliflower Soup

serves
6

2 x 400ml cans coconut milk

750ml (1¼ pints) vegetable stock

4 garlic cloves, finely chopped

5cm (2in) piece fresh root ginger,
    peeled and finely chopped

4 lemongrass stalks, roughly chopped

4 kaffir lime leaves, shredded
    (optional) or zest of 1 lime

4 red chillies

2 tbsp groundnut oil

2 tsp sesame oil

1 large onion, thinly sliced

2 tsp ground turmeric

2 tsp sugar

900g (2lb) cauliflower florets

2 tbsp lime juice

2 tbsp light soy sauce

4 spring onions, shredded

4 tbsp freshly chopped coriander

salt and ground black pepper

Pour the coconut milk and stock into a pan. Add the garlic and ginger with the lemongrass, lime leaves, if using, or lime zest and chillies. Bring to the boil, then reduce the heat, cover the pan and simmer for 15 minutes. Strain and keep the liquid to one side.

Heat the oils together in a clean saucepan. Add the onion, turmeric and sugar and fry gently for 5 minutes. Add the cauliflower to the pan and then stir-fry for 5 minutes or until lightly golden.

Add the reserved liquid, the lime juice and soy sauce. Bring to the boil, then reduce the heat, cover the pan and simmer gently for 10–15 minutes until the cauliflower is tender.

Season to taste with salt and pepper, then add the spring onions and coriander to the soup. Ladle into warmed bowls and serve.

Thai Chicken Broth

serves
4

1 tbsp olive oil
4 boneless skinless chicken thighs,
    around 300g (11oz), shredded
3 garlic cloves, roughly chopped
2 red chillies, seeded and finely diced
1 lemongrass stalk, finely sliced
5cm (2in) piece fresh root ginger,
    peeled and finely chopped
150ml (¼ pint) white wine
1 litre (1¾ pints) chicken stock

8 fresh coriander sprigs
50g (2oz) rice noodles
125g (4oz) green beans, trimmed
    and halved
125g (4oz) bean sprouts
4 spring onions, finely sliced
2 tbsp Thai fish sauce (nam pla)
juice of ½ lime
salt and ground black pepper

Heat the oil in a large pan over a medium heat. Add the chicken, garlic, chillies, lemongrass and ginger and cook for 3–5 minutes until the chicken is opaque.

Add the white wine and bring to the boil, then reduce the heat and simmer until reduced by half. Add the stock and bring to the boil. Simmer for 5 minutes or until the chicken is cooked through.

Pick the leaves off the coriander and put them to one side. Finely chop the stalks. Add the noodles to the pan and cook for 1 minute, then add the beans and coriander stalks. Cook for 3 minutes.

Add the bean sprouts and spring onions (reserving a few to garnish) along with the fish sauce and lime juice. Simmer until heated through, then taste for seasoning. Ladle the noodles and broth into warmed bowls, making sure that each serving has some chicken and bean sprouts. Garnish with the coriander leaves, spring onions and bean sprouts and serve.

Pork and Noodle Soup

serves
6

225g (8oz) minced pork
50g (2oz) peanuts or cashew nuts,
    roughly chopped
4 garlic cloves, crushed
2 tbsp freshly chopped coriander
1.7 litres (3 pints) chicken stock
3 lemongrass stalks, finely chopped
6 kaffir lime leaves, or zest of
    1 large lime
1 tbsp light soy sauce

1 tbsp Thai fish sauce
juice of 2 limes
1 tsp red curry paste or tandoori paste
2 tsp caster sugar
4 tbsp sunflower oil
125g (4oz) rice noodles or egg noodles
125g (4oz) mushrooms, sliced
125g (4oz) broccoli florets
salt and ground black pepper
lime wedges to serve

Put the pork into a bowl with the nuts, garlic and coriander and season to taste with salt and pepper. Mix thoroughly, then shape into 18 walnut-sized balls; knead thoroughly with your hands to help bind the mixture and prevent the meatballs breaking up during cooking.

Put the stock into a large saucepan with the lemongrass, lime leaves or grated rind, soy sauce, fish sauce, lime juice, curry paste and sugar. Bring to the boil, then reduce the heat, cover the pan and simmer for 20 minutes.

Meanwhile, heat 3 tbsp oil in a heavy-based frying pan and fry the meatballs in batches for 4–5 minutes or until golden and cooked through. Set aside.

Cook the noodles according to the packet instructions.

Meanwhile, heat the remaining oil in the frying pan and stir-fry the mushrooms and broccoli for 1–2 minutes. Drain the noodles and add to the pan with the meatballs. Strain the broth and combine with the pork and noodle mixture.

To serve, ladle the soup into warmed bowls and garnish with the lime wedges.

Spicy Beef and Noodle Soup

serves
4

15g (½oz) dried porcini or shiitake
    mushrooms
2 tbsp groundnut oil
225g (8oz) fillet steak, cut into thin
    strips
1.1 litres (2 pints) beef stock
2 tbsp Thai fish sauce (nam pla),
    plus extra if needed
1 large fresh red chilli, seeded and
    finely chopped
1 lemongrass stalk, trimmed and
    thinly sliced

2.5cm (1in) piece fresh root ginger,
    peeled and finely chopped
6 spring onions, halved lengthways
    and cut into 2.5cm (1in) lengths
1 garlic clove, crushed
¼ tsp caster sugar
50g (2oz) medium egg noodles
125g (4oz) fresh spinach leaves,
    roughly chopped
4 tbsp freshly chopped coriander
ground black pepper

Break the dried mushrooms into pieces and soak in 150ml (¼ pint) boiling water for 15 minutes.

Meanwhile, heat the oil in a large pan over a medium heat, brown the meat in two batches and put aside. Pour the stock into the pan with 2 tbsp fish sauce. Add the mushrooms and their soaking liquid, the chilli, lemongrass, ginger, spring onions, garlic and sugar and bring to the boil.

Break the noodles up slightly and add to the pan, then stir gently until they begin to separate. Simmer gently for 4–5 minutes until the noodles are just tender, stirring occasionally.

Stir in the spinach, coriander and reserved steak. Check and adjust the seasoning with black pepper and add a little more fish sauce if necessary. Ladle the soup into warmed bowls and serve hot.

Spicy Bean and Courgette Soup

serves
4

2 tbsp olive oil
175g (6oz) onions, finely chopped
2 garlic cloves, crushed
2 tsp ground coriander
1 tbsp paprika
1 tsp mild curry powder
450g (1lb) courgettes, trimmed,
   halved and sliced

225g (8oz) potatoes, peeled and diced
400g can red kidney beans, drained
   and rinsed
425g can flageolet beans, drained
   and rinsed
1.5 litres (2½ pints) vegetable stock
salt and ground black pepper
crusty bread to serve

Heat the oil in a saucepan. Add the onions and garlic and sauté for 2 minutes. Add the spices and curry powder and cook, stirring, for 1 minute. Mix in the courgettes and potatoes and cook for 1–2 minutes.

Add the remaining ingredients and bring to the boil, then reduce the heat, cover the pan and simmer for 25 minutes, stirring occasionally, or until the potatoes are tender. Adjust the seasoning if necessary.

Ladle the soup into warmed bowls and serve with crusty bread.

Cook's Tip
Courgettes are baby marrows. Look for small, firm vegetables. They lose their flavour as they grow larger.

Roasted Onion and Coconut Soup

serves
6

4 large onions, about 1.1kg (2½lb),
  halved
2 tsp olive oil
3 large red chillies
6 garlic cloves, unpeeled
½ tsp cumin seeds
900ml (1½ pints) vegetable or
  chicken stock
2 lemongrass stalks
3 kaffir lime leaves or zest of
  1 small lime
2 x 400ml cans coconut milk
salt and ground black pepper

For the Jamaican salsa
1 small banana (optional)
250g (8oz) plum tomatoes, quartered,
  seeded and finely chopped
1 green chilli, seeded and finely
  chopped
finely grated zest and juice of 1 lime
2 tbsp freshly chopped coriander
coriander, finely sliced red chilli and
  coconut milk to serve

Preheat the oven to 200°C (180°C fan oven) mark 6. Put the onions in a roasting tin and drizzle with oil. Cook for 20–30 minutes or until brown. Add the chillies, garlic and cumin seeds, cover with foil and cook for 40 minutes or until the onions are soft. Leave to cool.

Peel, halve and seed the chillies; discard the seeds. Squeeze the pulp from the garlic and discard the skins. Whiz the chillies, garlic and cooled onions in a food processor until smooth. Transfer the purée to a pan, add the stock, lemongrass and lime leaves or lime zest and season to taste with salt and pepper. Bring slowly to the boil, then reduce the heat, cover the pan and cook gently for 30 minutes.

For the salsa, peel the banana, if using, and chop into small pieces. Mix with the tomatoes, chilli, lime zest and juice and coriander.

Remove the lemongrass and lime leaves from the soup and discard. Stir in the coconut milk and heat gently. Ladle the soup into warmed serving bowls and add a spoonful of salsa, garnished with coriander, some §sliced chilli and a drizzle of coconut milk to each.

Curried Parsnip Soup

serves
6

40g (1½ oz) butter
1 onion, sliced
700g (1½lb) parsnips, peeled,
  cored and finely diced
1 tsp curry powder
½ tsp ground cumin

1.2 litres (2 pints) chicken or
  vegetable stock
150ml (¼ pint) single cream
salt and ground black pepper
paprika to sprinkle

Melt the butter in a large saucepan, add the onion and fry gently for 5–7 minutes.
Add the parsnips and fry gently for about 3 minutes.

Stir in the curry powder and cumin and cook for a further 2 minutes.

Add the stock, season to taste and bring to the boil. Reduce the heat, cover the
pan and simmer for 35 minutes or until the vegetables are tender.

Leave the soup to cool a little, then whiz in batches in a blender or food
processor until smooth. Return the soup to the pan and adjust the seasoning.
Add the cream and reheat but do not boil.

Ladle the soup into warmed bowls, sprinkle with paprika and serve.

Mexican Bean Soup

serves
6

4 tbsp olive oil
1 onion, chopped
2 garlic cloves, chopped
pinch of crushed red chillies
1 tsp ground coriander
1 tsp ground cumin
½ tsp ground cinnamon
900ml (1½ pints) vegetable stock
300ml (½ pint) tomato juice

1–2 tsp chilli sauce
2 x 400g cans red kidney beans
2 tbsp freshly chopped coriander
salt and ground black pepper
lime butter to serve (optional,
    see Cook's Tip)
coriander leaves, roughly torn,
    to garnish

Heat the oil in a large pan, add the onion, garlic, chilli and spices and fry gently for 5 minutes until lightly golden.

Add the stock, tomato juice, chilli sauce and beans with their liquid. Bring to the boil, then reduce the heat, cover the pan and simmer gently for 20 minutes.

Leave the soup to cool a little, then whiz in batches in a blender or food processor until very smooth. Return the soup to the pan. Stir in the chopped coriander and heat through, then season to taste with salt and pepper.

Ladle the soup into warmed bowls. Top each portion with a few slices of lime butter, if you like, and scatter with torn coriander leaves.

Cook's Tip
Lime Butter: Beat the grated zest and juice of ½ lime into 50g (2oz) softened butter and season to taste with salt and pepper. Shape into a log, wrap in some clingfilm and chill until needed. To serve, unwrap and slice thinly.

Mulligatawny Soup

3 rashers streaky bacon, rinded and
finely chopped
550g (1¼lb) chicken portions
600ml (1 pint) chicken stock
1 carrot, sliced
1 celery stick, chopped
1 apple, cored and chopped
2 tsp curry powder

4 peppercorns, crushed
1 clove
1 bay leaf
1 tbsp plain flour
150ml (¼ pint) milk
50g (2oz) long-grain rice, cooked,
and crusty bread to serve

Fry the bacon in a large saucepan until the fat begins to run. Do not allow the bacon to become brown.

Add the chicken and brown well. Drain the meat on some kitchen paper and pour off the fat.

Return the bacon and chicken to the pan and add the stock together with the next seven ingredients. Cover the pan and simmer for about 30 minutes or until the chicken is tender.

Remove the chicken and allow to cool a little. Cut off the meat and return it to the soup. Discard the clove and bay leaf and reheat the soup gently.

Mix the flour with a little cold water. Add to the soup with the milk and reheat, stirring with a wooden spoon, without boiling.

Ladle the soup into warmed bowls, spoon a mound of rice into each one and serve immediately with crusty bread.

Goulash Soup

700g (1½lb) silverside or lean chuck
  steak
25g (1oz) butter
225g (8oz) onions, chopped
1 small green pepper, seeded and
  chopped
4 tomatoes, skinned and quartered
150g (5oz) tomato purée

600ml (1 pint) rich beef stock
1 tbsp paprika
450g (1lb) potatoes, peeled
150ml (¼ pint) soured cream
salt and ground black pepper
freshly chopped parsley to garnish
  (optional)

Wipe the meat with a damp cloth. Remove any excess fat or gristle and cut the meat into small pieces. Season well with 2 tsp salt and pepper to taste.

Melt the butter in a large saucepan, add the onions and green pepper and sauté until tender.

Add the meat pieces, tomatoes, tomato purée, stock and paprika. Stir well and bring to the boil, then reduce the heat, cover the pan and simmer for 2½ hours, stirring occasionally.

Half an hour before the end of cooking, cut the potatoes into bite-size pieces, bring to the boil in a pan of lightly salted water and then simmer until cooked. Drain well and add to the soup.

Check the seasoning and stir in 2 tbsp soured cream. Ladle into warmed bowls, garnish with chopped parsley, if you like, and serve the remaining soured cream separately, for each person to spoon into their soup.

Hot and Sour Soup

serves
4

1 tbsp vegetable oil
2 turkey breasts, about 300g (11oz),
    or the same quantity of tofu,
    cut into strips
5cm (2in) piece fresh root ginger,
    peeled and grated
4 spring onions, finely sliced
1–2 tbsp Thai red curry paste

75g (3oz) long-grain wild rice
1.1 litres (2 pints) hot weak chicken
    or vegetable stock or boiling water
200g (7oz) mangetouts, sliced
juice of 1 lime
4 tbsp roughly chopped fresh coriander
    to garnish

Heat the oil in a deep saucepan. Add the turkey or tofu and cook over a medium heat for 5 minutes or until browned. Add the ginger and spring onions and cook for a further 2–3 minutes. Stir in the curry paste and cook for 1–2 minutes to warm the spices.

Add the rice and stir to coat in the curry paste. Pour the hot stock or boiling water into the pan. Stir once and bring to the boil, then reduce the heat, cover the pan and simmer for 20 minutes.

Add the mangetouts and cook for a further 5 minutes or until the rice is cooked. Just before serving, squeeze in the lime juice and stir to mix.

To serve, ladle into warmed bowls and sprinkle with the coriander.

Spiced Dal Soup

serves
4

125g (4oz) chana dal
1 tsp cumin seeds
2 tsp coriander seeds
1 tsp fenugreek seeds
3 dried red chillies
1 tbsp shredded coconut
2 tbsp ghee or polyunsaturated oil

225g (8oz) tomatoes, skinned and
    roughly chopped
½ tsp turmeric
1 tsp treacle
coriander sprigs to garnish
lemon wedges to serve

Pick over the dal and remove any grit or discoloured pulses. Put into a sieve and wash in cold running water, then drain well and put into a saucepan. Cover with 600ml (1 pint) water and bring to the boil, then reduce the heat, cover the pan and simmer for 1 hour or until tender.

Put the cumin, coriander, fenugreek, chillies and coconut into a small electric mill or blender and grind finely. Heat the oil in a heavy-based frying pan, add the spice mixture and fry, stirring, for 30 seconds. Whiz the dal to a purée in a blender or food processor and put into a pan. Stir in the remaining ingredients and 300ml (½ pint) water.

Bring to the boil, then reduce the heat, cover the pan and simmer gently for about 20 minutes. Taste and adjust the seasoning. To serve, ladle into warmed bowls and garnish with coriander sprigs, with lemon wedges to squeeze in.

Green Lentil and Coconut Soup

225g (8oz) whole green lentils
4 tbsp sunflower oil
350g (12oz) floury potatoes,
   peeled and diced
1 large onion, chopped
2 garlic cloves, crushed
¼ tsp ground turmeric
2 tsp ground cumin

50g (2oz) creamed coconut
750ml (1¼ pints) vegetable stock
300ml (½ pint) coconut milk
finely grated zest of 1 lemon
salt and ground black pepper
toasted fresh coconut and coriander
   sprigs (optional) to garnish

Put the lentils into a sieve and wash them thoroughly under cold running water. Drain well.

Heat the oil in a large pan. Add the potatoes and fry gently for 5 minutes until beginning to colour. Remove with a slotted spoon and drain on kitchen paper.

Add the onion to the pan and fry gently for 10 minutes until soft. Add the garlic, turmeric and cumin and fry for 2–3 minutes. Add the coconut, stock, coconut milk and lentils and bring to the boil, then reduce the heat, cover the pan and simmer gently for 20 minutes until the lentils are just tender.

Add the potatoes and lemon zest and season to taste with salt and pepper. Cook gently for 5 minutes until the potatoes are tender. Ladle into warmed bowls, garnish with toasted coconut and the coriander sprigs, if you like, and serve hot.

Curried Mussel Soup

serves 4

2kg (4½lb) fresh mussels in shells, cleaned
90ml (3fl oz) dry white wine
a pinch of saffron strands
450ml (¾ pint) hot fish or vegetable stock
25g (1oz) butter
4 shallots, finely chopped
1 garlic clove, crushed

1 tsp grated fresh root ginger
½ tsp ground turmeric
½ tsp garam masala
150ml (¼ pint) double cream
1 tbsp freshly chopped parsley or chervil
1 tsp lemon juice, or to taste
ground black pepper
warm crusty bread to serve (optional)

Put the mussels into a large pan with the wine. Cover with a tight-fitting lid and steam for 4–5 minutes until the shells have opened, shaking the pan frequently; discard any mussels that remain closed.

Meanwhile, put the saffron strands into a bowl, pour on the hot stock and leave to infuse for about 10 minutes.

Strain the mussel liquor through a muslin-lined sieve and set aside. Shell the mussels, keeping eight in their shells for the garnish.

Melt the butter in a pan, add the shallots, garlic, ginger, turmeric and garam masala and fry gently for 5 minutes until the shallots are soft but not golden. Add the saffron stock and mussel liquor and simmer gently, uncovered, for 10 minutes.

Stir in the cream, shelled mussels and parsley or chervil and heat through. Add the lemon juice and season to taste with black pepper.

Ladle the soup into warmed bowls and top with the reserved mussels in shells. Serve with warm crusty bread, if you like.

Chilled soups

Iced Sweet Pepper Soup

**serves
4**

4 tbsp freshly chopped coriander
2 medium red peppers, seeded and
  sliced
1 medium onion, sliced

225g (8oz) ripe tomatoes, sliced
900ml (1½ pints) vegetable stock
150ml (¼ pint) milk
salt and ground black pepper

First make the coriander ice cubes. Put the chopped coriander into an ice-cube tray, top up with water and freeze.

Put the peppers into a large saucepan with the onion, tomatoes and stock. Bring to the boil, then lower the heat, cover the pan and simmer for about 15 minutes or until the vegetables are tender. Drain, reserving the liquid.

Whiz the vegetables in a blender or food processor until smooth, then sieve the purée to remove the tomato seeds.

Combine the reserved liquid, vegetable purée and milk in a bowl with salt and pepper to taste. Cool for 30 minutes, then chill for at least 2 hours before serving. Ladle the soup into chilled bowls and serve with coriander ice cubes.

Chilled Avocado and Lime Soup

serves 4

1 tbsp extra virgin olive oil
1 bunch of spring onions, trimmed
    and sliced
225g (8oz) potatoes, peeled and
    cubed
900ml (1½ pints) vegetable stock

1-2 limes
2 ripe avocados
salt and ground black pepper
snipped chives to garnish
6 bsp very low-fat fromage frais and
    Melba Toast (see page 60) to serve

Heat the oil in a large pan, add the spring onions and fry gently until softened.

Add the potatoes to the pan and fry, stirring, for 2 minutes. Add the stock and bring to the boil, then reduce the heat, cover the pan and simmer gently for 15–20 minutes.

Towards the end of the cooking time, remove a little zest from one of the limes, using a zester, and set aside for the garnish. Squeeze the juice from the lime. Halve, stone and peel the avocados, then chop roughly. Add the avocado to the soup with the lime juice. Taste and adjust the seasoning; add extra lime juice (from the other lime) if required.

Remove the soup from the heat, allow to cool a little, then whiz in a blender or food processor until smooth. Add 2 tbsp fromage frais and stir to mix. Ladle into soup bowls and chill for 3–4 hours. (The soup thickens as it is chilled.)

To serve, add a swirl of fromage frais and a squeeze of lime juice to each bowl. Grind some black pepper on top and garnish with snipped chives and the lime zest. Serve with Melba Toast.

Chilled Pea Soup with Mint Salsa

serves 4

450g (1lb) fresh peas in their pods
2 tbsp olive oil
2 leeks, trimmed and sliced
1 garlic clove, crushed
175g (6oz) potato, peeled and cubed
1 litre (1¾ pints) vegetable stock
150ml (¼ pint) double cream
salt and ground black pepper
mint sprigs to garnish

For the mint salsa
juice of 1 lemon
25g (1oz) golden caster sugar
1 small onion, finely chopped
125g (4oz) cucumber, peeled,
 seeded and diced
4 tbsp freshly chopped mint

Remove the peas from their pods, reserving both peas and pods. String the pods and cut into pieces.

Heat the oil in a saucepan, add the leeks, garlic and pea pods and fry gently for 5 minutes. Add the potato and stock and bring to the boil, then reduce the heat, cover the pan and simmer gently for 20 minutes.

Leave the soup to cool a little, then whiz in batches in a blender or food processor until smooth. Pass through a fine sieve into the cleaned pan and stir in the fresh peas. Cover and cook gently for a further 10 minutes until the peas are tender.

Meanwhile, make the salsa. Put the lemon juice and sugar into a small pan and heat gently to dissolve. Add the onion, cucumber and a pinch of salt. Remove from the heat, stir in the chopped mint and set aside to cool.

Season the soup with salt and pepper, cool, then chill for several hours.

To serve, stir the cream into the soup and adjust the seasoning. Ladle into bowls and top with the salsa and mint sprigs, adding a few ice cubes, if you like.

Cook's Tip
The pea pods add a depth of flavour and richness to the soup.

Cucumber, Yogurt and Mint Soup

serves 6

1 cucumber, coarsely grated
500g (1lb 2oz) Greek yogurt
a generous handful of mint leaves,
   chopped
1 large garlic clove, crushed

125ml (4fl oz) cold water or light
   vegetable or chicken stock
salt and ground black pepper
6 ice cubes and mint sprigs to serve

Set aside 6 tbsp of the cucumber. Put the remainder into a large bowl with all the remaining ingredients for the soup and mix together. Chill until required.

Before serving, stir the soup, then taste and adjust the seasoning. Spoon the soup into six bowls and drop an ice cube, 1 tbsp of the reserved cucumber and a few mint sprigs into each bowl.

Health Tip
Raw garlic: This is a wonderful tonic for your health and is world-renowned for its curative and protective powers, including lowering blood pressure and cholesterol levels.
Fresh garlic: With its plump, juicy, mild cloves, this is available from May onwards throughout the summer. It is the classic form of garlic to use for making pesto, salsa verde, garlic mayonnaise and chilled soups.

Chilled Leek and Potato Soup with Prawns and Spinach Cream

serves 4

1kg (2¼lb) trimmed leeks, chopped
50g (2oz) butter
350g (12oz) onions, roughly chopped
1.1 litres (2 pints) vegetable stock
140ml (4½fl oz) double cream
225g (8oz) potatoes, peeled and sliced
salt and ground black pepper
cooked peeled prawns and fresh basil
    sprigs to garnish

For the spinach cream
15g (½oz) butter
125g (4oz) spinach leaves
zest of 1 lemon
140ml (4½fl oz) double cream

Rinse the leeks in cold water, drain and set aside. Melt the butter in a large heavy-based pan and add the onions and leeks. Cook, stirring, for 10 minutes. Add the stock, cream and potatoes and bring to the boil, then reduce the heat, cover the pan and simmer for 30–40 minutes until the vegetables are tender.

Leave the soup to cool a little, then whiz in batches in a blender or food processor until smooth. Pass through a fine sieve if you like, then season well with salt and pepper. Chill for 6 hours or overnight.

Meanwhile, to make the spinach cream, heat the butter in a pan, then add the spinach and lemon zest. Cook, stirring, for 5 minutes. Add the cream and bubble for 1–2 minutes. Whiz in a blender or food processor until smooth. Season to taste with salt and pepper, then chill.

Ladle the soup into chilled bowls and spoon in the spinach cream. Garnish with prawns and basil, sprinkle with black pepper and serve.

Iced Tomato and Herb Soup

serves 4

450g (1lb) ripe tomatoes
1 small onion, sliced
4 tsp tomato purée
400g can chicken consommé
2 tbsp freshly chopped herbs, such
    as basil, coriander, parsley

25g (1oz) fresh white breadcrumbs
150ml (¼ pint) soured cream
salt and ground black pepper
fresh basil leaves to garnish

Roughly chop the tomatoes and whiz in a blender or food processor with the onion, tomato purée, consommé and herbs until smooth.

Rub the tomato mixture through a nylon sieve into a saucepan. Heat through gently to remove the frothy texture, then add plenty of salt and pepper.

Pour the soup into a large serving bowl and stir in the breadcrumbs. Chill in the refrigerator for at least 2 hours.

To serve, stir the soured cream until smooth, then swirl into the soup. Float the fresh basil leaves on top and serve immediately.

Chilled Asparagus Soup

serves
6

1.1kg (2½lb) asparagus, trimmed
3 tbsp olive oil
4 large shallots, finely chopped
200g (7oz) leeks, trimmed and finely
    chopped
salt and ground black pepper
chervil sprigs to serve

Cut the tips off the asparagus stems and set them aside. Cut the asparagus stalks into 2.5cm (1in) lengths.

Heat the oil in a large saucepan, add the shallots and cook gently over a low heat for 2–3 minutes. Add the leeks and cook, stirring occasionally, for 10 minutes or until they are soft.

Add the asparagus stalks and 900ml (1½ pints) water and season to taste with salt and pepper. Bring to the boil, then reduce the heat and simmer very gently, uncovered, for 10 minutes or until the asparagus is soft.

Leave the soup to cool a little, then whiz in a blender or food processor until smooth. Pour into a bowl and set aside to cool.

Add the asparagus tips to a saucepan of lightly salted boiling water and cook for 2–3 minutes until tender. Drain and refresh under cold running water.

Add the asparagus tips to the soup, cover and chill for several hours.

To serve, stir about 450ml (¾ pint) iced water into the soup to obtain the required consistency. Season generously with salt and pepper. Ladle the soup into chilled bowls, top with chervil and serve.

Gazpacho with Tortilla Chips

serves 8

900g (2lb) ripe tomatoes
4 garlic cloves
50g (2oz) fresh white breadcrumbs
6 tbsp extra virgin olive oil
juice of 1½ small limes
1 red chilli, seeded and chopped
2 cucumbers, seeded and chopped
2 bunches of spring onions, chopped
1 red pepper, seeded and chopped
600ml (1 pint) tomato juice

6 tbsp freshly chopped coriander
salt and ground black pepper
175g bag tortilla chips to serve

To garnish
1 large avocado
juice of ½ small lime
140ml (4½fl oz) soured cream
a few fresh coriander sprigs

Score a cross in the skin at the base of each tomato, then put in a bowl. Pour over enough boiling water to cover them, leave for 30 seconds, then transfer to a bowl of cold water. Peel, discarding the skins. Cut into quarters. Discard the seeds.

Put all the gazpacho ingredients into a large bowl and mix well, then whiz together in batches in a blender or food processor until smooth. Transfer to a bowl or jug, season to taste generously with salt and pepper and stir the soup well. Cover and chill for at least 2 hours or overnight.

Just before serving, peel and roughly dice the avocado, then toss in lime juice to coat. Ladle the soup into chilled bowls and garnish with soured cream, the avocado, a sprinkling of black pepper and coriander sprigs. Hand round the tortilla chips separately.

Roasted Vegetable Soup with Olive and Basil Cream

serves 8

1.4kg (3lb) ripe tomatoes, halved
350g (12oz) shallots or onions, halved
275g (10oz) celery, chopped
4 small garlic cloves
275g (10oz) carrots, sliced
4 red peppers, seeded and chopped
4 tbsp olive oil
2 red chillies

750ml (1¼ pints) passata
    (see Cook's Tips)
1½ tsp sugar
grated zest and juice of 1 lime
salt and ground black pepper
crushed ice and Olive and Basil Cream
    (see Cook's Tips) to serve

Preheat the oven to 200°C (180°C fan oven) mark 6. Divide all the vegetables between two roasting tins. Add the oil and chillies, then stir well. Roast for 1–1½ hours or until the skins are charred, turning halfway through the cooking time.

Discard the chillies. Whiz the vegetables with the passata in a blender or food processor until smooth, then push the purée through a sieve.

Add the sugar, lime zest and 2 tbsp juice and some seasoning. Cover and chill.

Ladle the soup into chilled bowls, sprinkle with crushed ice and top with Olive and Basil Cream.

Cook's Tips
Passata: A mixture of sieved tomatoes rather like tomato paste, this is sold in cartons and bottles. Look out for it in supermarkets.
Olive and Basil Cream: Roughly chop 50g (2oz) pitted black olives. Stir into 150ml (¼ pint) crème fraîche with 2 tbsp freshly chopped basil and the grated zest and juice of 1 lemon. Season well with salt and ground black pepper. Cover and chill the cream until ready to serve, then spoon on to the soup.

Iced Courgette Soup

serves 4

50g (2oz) butter or margarine
450g (1lb) courgettes, trimmed and
 chopped
1 medium potato, peeled and diced
750ml (1¼ pints) vegetable stock
 or water

1 tsp freshly chopped basil
 or ½ tsp dried basil
125g (4oz) ripe Blue Brie
salt and ground black pepper
sliced courgettes to serve (optional)

Melt the butter or margarine in a large heavy-based saucepan. Add the courgettes
and potato, cover the pan and fry gently for about 10 minutes until softened,
shaking the pan frequently.

Add the stock or water with the basil and season to taste with salt and pepper.
Bring to the boil, stirring, then reduce the heat and simmer for 20 minutes until
the vegetables are tender.

Remove the rind from the Brie and chop the cheese into small dice. Put into a
blender or food processor, then pour in the soup and whiz until smooth. Turn
into a bowl, cover and leave until cold. Chill in the refrigerator overnight.

Whisk the soup vigorously to ensure an even consistency, then taste and adjust
the seasoning. Ladle into a chilled soup tureen or individual bowls and float the
courgette slices on the top, if you like.

Chilled Beetroot and Apple Soup

serves 4

350g (12oz) cooked, peeled beetroot, cut into chunks
juice of ½ lemon
600ml (1 pint) unsweetened apple juice, chilled
200g (7oz) Greek yogurt, chilled

cayenne pepper
10cm (4in) piece cucumber
1 tbsp freshly chopped mint, plus mint sprigs to garnish
salt and ground black pepper

Put the beetroot into a food processor with the lemon juice, half the apple juice and half the yogurt. Whiz for 1–2 minutes until smooth, then press through a sieve into a bowl.

Stir in the remaining apple juice, and season to taste with cayenne, salt and pepper. Chill in the refrigerator.

When ready to serve, grate the cucumber into the remaining yogurt and stir in the mint. Ladle the soup into serving bowls and stir some cucumber yogurt into the middle of each. Sprinkle with a little cayenne pepper, if you like, garnish with mint leaves and serve.

Feel good soups

Autumn Barley Soup

serves 4

25g (1oz) pot barley, washed and drained
1 litre (1¾ pints) vegetable stock
2 large carrots, diced
1 turnip, peeled and diced
2 leeks, trimmed and sliced
2 celery sticks, diced

1 small onion, finely chopped
1 bouquet garni (1 bay leaf, a sprig each of thyme and parsley and a celery stick)
ground black pepper
2 tbsp freshly chopped parsley
salt and ground black pepper

Put the barley and stock into a saucepan and bring to the boil. Reduce the heat and simmer for 45 minutes until tender.

Add the vegetables to the pan with the bouquet garni and season to taste with black pepper. Bring to the boil, then reduce the heat and simmer gently for about 20 minutes or until the vegetables are tender.

Discard the bouquet garni. Add the parsley to the soup, season to taste with salt and pepper and stir well, then ladle into warmed bowls and serve immediately.

Chicken and Bean Soup

serves
4

1 tbsp olive oil
1 onion, finely chopped
4 celery sticks, chopped
1 red chilli, seeded and roughly
    chopped
2 skinless chicken breasts,
    cut into strips
1 litre (1¾ pints) hot chicken
    or vegetable stock

100g (3½oz) bulgur wheat
2 x 400g cans cannellini beans,
    drained
400g can chopped tomatoes
25g (1oz) flat-leafed parsley, roughly
    chopped
wholegrain bread and hummus to
    serve

Heat the oil in a large heavy-based saucepan. Add the onion, celery and chilli
and cook over a low heat for 10 minutes or until softened. Add the chicken and
stir-fry for 3–4 minutes until golden.

Add the hot stock to the pan and bring to a simmer. Stir in the bulgur wheat and
simmer for 15 minutes, then stir in the cannellini beans and tomatoes and return
to a simmer.

Sprinkle the chopped parsley over the soup and ladle into warmed serving bowls.
Serve with wholegrain bread and hummus.

Chicken Broth

1 tbsp olive oil
about 300g (11oz) boneless skinless
  chicken thighs, cubed
3 garlic cloves, crushed
2 medium red chillies, seeded and
  finely diced

1 litre (1¾ pints) chicken stock
250g (9oz) each green beans, broccoli,
  sugarsnap peas and courgettes,
  chopped
50g (2oz) pasta shapes or spaghetti,
  broken into short lengths

Heat the oil in a large saucepan, add the chicken, garlic and chillies and cook for 5–10 minutes or until the chicken is opaque all over.

Add the stock and bring to the boil, then add the vegetables, reduce the heat and simmer for 5 minutes or until the chicken is cooked through.

Meanwhile, cook the pasta in a separate pan of lightly salted boiling water until just cooked, about 5–10 minutes, depending on the type of pasta.

Drain the pasta and add to the broth. Ladle the soup into warmed bowls and serve immediately.

Full-of-goodness Broth

serves 4

1–2 tbsp medium curry paste
200ml (7fl oz) reduced-fat coconut
   milk
600ml (1 pint) hot vegetable stock
200g (7oz) smoked tofu, cubed

2 pak choi, chopped
a handful of sugarsnap peas
4 spring onions, chopped
lime wedges to serve

Heat the curry paste in a saucepan for 1–2 minutes. Add the coconut milk and hot stock and bring to the boil.

Add the smoked tofu, pak choi, sugarsnap peas and spring onions, then reduce the heat and simmer for 1–2 minutes.

Ladle the soup into warmed bowls and serve with a wedge of lime to squeeze in.

Try Something Different
You can replace the smoked tofu with shredded leftover roast chicken and simmer for 2–3 minutes.

Cream of Parsley Soup

serves
8

50g (2oz) butter or polyunsaturated
  margarine
225g (8oz) parsley, roughly chopped
2 medium onions, sliced
125g (4oz) celery, sliced

3 tbsp plain wholemeal flour
2 litres (3½ pints) vegetable stock
150ml (¼ pint) single cream
salt and ground black pepper
parsley sprigs to garnish

Melt the butter or margarine in a large saucepan and add the parsley, onions and celery. Cover the pan and cook gently for about 10 minutes until the vegetables are soft. Shake the pan occasionally.

Stir in the flour until smooth, then mix in the stock. Add salt and pepper to taste and bring to the boil, then reduce the heat, cover the pan and simmer gently for 25–30 minutes.

Leave the soup to cool a little, then whiz in batches in a blender or food processor until smooth. Leave to cool completely, then chill.

Reheat until bubbling, then taste and adjust the seasoning and swirl in the cream. Ladle the soup into warmed bowls, garnish with parsley sprigs and serve.

Mushroom, Spinach and Miso Soup

serves 6

1 tbsp vegetable oil
1 onion, finely sliced
125g (4oz) shiitake mushrooms,
    finely sliced

225g (8oz) baby spinach leaves
1.1 litres (2 pints) fresh fish stock
4 tbsp mugi miso (see Cook's Tip)

Heat the oil in a large saucepan over a low heat, add the onion and cook gently for 15 minutes until soft.

Add the mushrooms and cook for 5 minutes, then stir in the spinach and stock. Heat for 3 minutes, then stir in the miso – don't boil, as miso is a live culture. Ladle the soup into warmed bowls and serve hot.

Cook's Tip
Miso (fermented barley and soya beans) is a living food in the same way that yogurt is and contains bacteria and enzymes that are destroyed by boiling. Miso is best added as a flavouring at the end of cooking. It's available from most Asian shops and larger supermarkets.

Spinach and Rice Soup

4 tbsp extra virgin olive oil, plus extra
    to serve
1 onion, finely chopped
2 garlic cloves, crushed
2 tsp freshly chopped thyme or
    a large pinch of dried thyme
2 tsp freshly chopped rosemary or
    a large pinch of dried rosemary
zest of ½ lemon

2 tsp ground coriander
¼ tsp cayenne pepper
125g (4oz) arborio rice
1.1 litres (2 pints) vegetable stock
225g (8oz) fresh or frozen and thawed
    spinach, shredded
4 tbsp pesto
salt and ground black pepper
freshly grated Parmesan to serve

Heat half the oil in a saucepan. Add the onion, garlic, herbs, lemon zest and spices, then fry gently for 5 minutes.

Add the remaining oil with the rice and cook, stirring with a wooden spoon, for 1 minute. Add the stock and bring to the boil, then reduce the heat and simmer gently for 20 minutes or until the rice is tender.

Stir the spinach into the soup with the pesto. Cook for 2 minutes, then season to taste with salt and pepper.

Ladle the soup into warmed bowls and serve drizzled with a little oil and topped with grated Parmesan.

Spring Vegetable Broth

serves
4

1 tbsp olive oil
4 shallots, chopped
1 fennel bulb, chopped
1 leek, trimmed and chopped
5 small carrots, chopped
1.1 litres (2 pints) hot chicken stock

2 courgettes, chopped
1 bunch of asparagus, chopped
2 x 400g cans cannellini beans, drained
   and rinsed
50g (2oz) Gruyère or Parmesan cheese
   shavings to serve

Heat the oil in a large saucepan. Add the shallots, fennel, leek and carrots and fry for 5 minutes or until they start to soften.

Add the hot stock, then cover the pan and bring to the boil. Add the courgettes, asparagus and beans, then reduce the heat and simmer for 5–6 minutes until the vegetables are tender.

Ladle the soup into warmed bowls, sprinkle with a little cheese and serve.

Variation
This broth is also good served with a tablespoon of pesto added to each bowl and served with chunks of crusty bread.

Celery Soup

serves 4

25g (1oz) butter
1 tbsp olive oil
1 medium leek, trimmed and sliced
6 celery sticks, finely sliced
1 tbsp finely chopped sage

600ml (1 pint) hot chicken stock
300ml (½ pint) milk
salt and ground black pepper
basil sprigs to garnish

Melt the butter in a pan and add the oil. Add the leek and fry for 10–15 minutes until soft. Add the celery and sage and cook for 5 minutes to soften.

Add the hot stock and milk to the pan, then season with salt and pepper, cover and bring to the boil. Reduce the heat and simmer for 10–15 minutes until the celery is tender.

Leave the soup to cool a little, then whiz in batches in a blender or food processor until smooth. Return the soup to the pan, reheat gently and season to taste with salt and pepper.

Ladle the soup into warmed serving bowls, sprinkle with black pepper, garnish with basil sprigs and serve.

Try Something Different
Instead of celery, use 500g (1lb 2oz) celeriac, peeled and diced. Replace the sage with 2 tsp freshly chopped thyme.

Herb and Lemon Soup

serves 6

1.7 litres (3 pints) chicken stock
150g (5oz) orzo or other dried
   soup pasta
3 medium eggs
juice of 1 large lemon

2 tbsp finely chopped fresh chives
2 tbsp finely chopped fresh chervil
salt and ground black pepper
lemon wedges to serve

Bring the stock to the boil in a large pan. Add the pasta and cook for 5 minutes or according to the packet instructions.

Beat the eggs in a bowl until frothy, then add the lemon juice and 1 tbsp cold water. Slowly stir in two ladlefuls of the hot stock. Put the egg mixture into the pan with the rest of the stock, then warm through gently over a very low heat for about 2–3 minutes.

Add the chives and chervil and season with salt and pepper. Ladle the soup into warmed bowls and serve immediately, with lemon wedges.

Cook's Tip
Once you have added the eggs, don't boil the soup or the eggs will curdle.

Summer Vegetable Soup with Pistou

**serves
6**

3 tbsp sunflower oil

1 onion, finely chopped

225g (8oz) waxy potatoes, peeled
and finely diced

175g (6oz) carrots, finely diced

1 medium turnip, finely diced

4 bay leaves

6 large fresh sage leaves

2 courgettes, about 375g (13oz), diced

175g (6oz) green beans, trimmed and
halved

125g (4oz) shelled small peas

225g (8oz) tomatoes, seeded and finely
diced

1 small broccoli head, broken into florets

salt and ground black pepper

Pistou (see Cook's Tip) or ready-made
pesto to serve

Heat the oil in a large pan over a gentle heat. Add the onion, potatoes, carrots
and turnip and cook for 10 minutes. Pour in 1.7 litres (3 pints) cold water and
season with salt and pepper. Bring to the boil and add the bay and sage leaves,
then reduce the heat and simmer for 25 minutes.

Add the courgettes, beans, peas and tomatoes. Bring back to the boil, then
reduce the heat and simmer for 10–15 minutes. Add the broccoli 5 minutes
before the end of the cooking time.

Remove the bay and sage leaves and adjust the seasoning. Ladle the soup into
warmed bowls and serve immediately, with the pistou or pesto on the side to stir
into the hot soup.

Cook's Tip

Pistou is a Provençal condiment that is similar to Italian pesto. To make your
own, using a pestle and mortar, or a small bowl and the end of a rolling pin, or
a mini processor, pound together ¾ tsp sea salt and 6 chopped garlic cloves until
smooth. Add 15g (½oz) freshly chopped basil and pound to a paste, then mix in
12 tbsp olive oil, a little at a time. You can store the pistou in a sealed jar in the
refrigerator for up to one week.

Lettuce Soup

serves 4

50g (2oz) butter
350g (12oz) lettuce leaves, roughly
   chopped
125g (4oz) spring onions, trimmed and
   roughly chopped

1 tbsp plain wholemeal flour
600ml (1 pint) vegetable stock
150ml (1/4 pint) milk
salt and ground black pepper
soured cream to serve (optional)

Melt the butter in a deep saucepan, add the lettuce and spring onions and cook gently for about
10 minutes until very soft.

Stir in the flour and cook, stirring, for 1 minute, then add the stock. Bring to the boil, then reduce the heat, cover the pan and simmer for 45 minutes to 1 hour.

Leave the soup to cool a little, when whiz in batches in a blender or food processor until smooth. Return to the rinsed-out pan and add the milk with salt and pepper to taste. Reheat to serving temperature.

Ladle into warmed bowls and finish with a swirl of soured cream, if you like.

Index